BLACKED OUT:

Religion & Racism

How People of Color were removed
from the pages of Biblical History

ESAAC ISRAEL

BLACKED OUT: Religion & Racism
How People of Color were removed from the pages of Biblical History

Esaac Israel

Pleasant Plant
1227 Rockbridge Rd
Suite 208-60
Stone Mountain GA 30087

Editor
Lael Israel

ISBN:　　　　　978-0-9988333-0-9

Library of Congress Control Number: 2017939996

DEDICATION

This book is dedicated to my mentor Elder Priest Yachov Ben Yisrael. I wish you were here now, but I wouldn't be the me that I am supposed to be if you were. I thank you for pushing me out of my comfort zone. I thank you for telling me even the intimate details of your successes and your failures. I thank you for also not revealing all the answers to me. You made me work for it and I love you for it. As It is written "…your eyes shall behold your teachers." I can't wait to hear you say again "Read Brother".

Shalom

Soc

CONTENTS

BLACKED OUT:
Religion & Racism

How People of color were removed from the pages of Biblical History

I must begin by saying that in years past I would have labeled myself the most unlikely source of any biblical commentary. In fact, someone close to me once stated that I would make songs about the bible someday. I quickly put them in their place with choice words. Years later, I had to offer them an apology, as they were right. In fact, I wrote many songs about the bible. But in my own defense, there was absolutely nothing about my hard core raps or vulgar standup comedy routines, that would make one say, hey, that guy will grow up to be a priest someday.

I always had a love and zeal for God, even though knowledge about anything concerning The Most High was in short supply. My family was spiritual, but not biblical. It would be years later before I would understand what this statement meant. To many black families, church is the only answer we have, no matter what the question is. In most families, there is one main figure that holds everything together and demands order. In my family, it was my grandfather. His father started a church which has grown to be one of the biggest in the Atlanta area. My grandfather died when I was young, and the attention for attendance on Sunday morning died with him.

Although there is a large monstrosity of a church building that owes its existence to my great grandfather, I can't remember ever going there. What I remember is accompanying my mother to a small house that was converted to a church of some sort. The church was owned and operated by a woman who lived up the street from my childhood home. It seemed to serve mostly women, and all consultations were in private. I don't remember ever seeing a bible there, just lots of candles. I guess it's safe to say that it was more of a private prayer service than it was a church.

SEARCHING FOR A
CHURCH HOME

It is said that you should raise a child in the way that they should go, and when they are grown they will not depart. The biggest part of this statement is, when they are grown. There is a stage in our lives where we bask in our new found independence, but are not yet grown. It's this gray area, where we act like puppies that have never been outside, performing deeds that we will not be proud of later. That being said, as I got older and came into my own, I started to search for a church home.

As with most things, I started and stopped a time or two but eventually I found a church home and was happy. As I began to be more comfortable, I opened up a little more. My zeal for The Most High caused me to shed tears on many occasions. It seemed to be that the way to show your love for GOD was to have emotional outbursts. I knew that I didn't understand Biblical concepts, but I knew how to cry, and boy did I do it. Sometimes I needed Gatorade from all the fluids I lost from crying and sweating. But what else was I to do, I didn't know anything, so it was my only avenue. I finally decided that there must be more to God's love than just me crying, so I began to read just a little. I began to grow and It was great, but then the let down came. I must have prayed a little too much, because then came a little understanding. The more I learned, the more I was confused. What I learned was not biblical concepts, what I learned was the order of service and how things went. I had spiritually hit the ceiling! I was able to finish the sermons myself, and I didn't know anything! This troubled me, but not enough to leave. What really troubled me was when I learned that when certain music was played, that certain of the same individuals would CATCH THE SPIRIT, and even pass out, on queue. I learned that the music was an effective tool to pull emotions out of people, sort of like a theatrical score.

THE PASS OUT

On one particular Sunday morning I was more emotional than usual. The set up for services was different this week. This week there was a guest preacher present. He was requesting individuals to come to the front of the church with a special offering. The special offering amount was $1000 dollars.

I sat in my seat because I figured that was too steep for me, but eventually I came down to the front of the church with my offering. Each person received a personal prophecy in front of the congregation for their offering. As the guest preacher made his way down the line, I noticed that there was a person behind each individual as he prayed and prophesied over each one of them. As he went from person to person they all passed out one by one. As they came closer toward me I began to realize the purpose of the person behind each individual.

His job was to catch the person as they passed out. So far every single person passed out! As he got to me, he put his hand over my head and gently squeezed my temples and rocked my head back and forth, as if he was intentionally attempting to make me dizzy. Then the role of the person behind me became crystal clear. He was not there to catch me. His job was to make sure I would fall back. As the one in front of me rocked my head back and forth, the one in the back gently pulled my underarms backward; basically instructing me to lie down and he would guide me to the floor. As he pulled me from the back, I pulled my body back forward. As it became apparent to them that I was not going to fall down, the guest preacher glanced at the regular preacher and then looked back at me. He then said some basic words over me, absolutely nothing like the rest, and went on to the next person. I felt numb afterwards. I later found out that there was nothing special about my event. Sometime later I spoke to two other people who had experienced the same thing, and both at different churches. One was a man, the other was a woman. The man stated that he refused to go along with the plan and pass out as well. The woman said she went along with the unspoken plan and pretended to pass out. Her mother also confessed to me that she was present when her daughter pretended to pass out, and she didn't believe it for one second. So she decided to walk down close to her daughter and noticed her daughter open one eye and peak at her mother.

SERMON PREACHED INCORRECTLY

Having some disenchantment about my episode, I stopped going to church for a small span. In that time I did a little reading and in the process I read one bible story completely. I must explain that I was never much of a reader. I mean I read well, but I never did recreational reading. I read to pass a particular test, and after that was done I would never pick up that book again. So needless to say, this was quite an accomplishment for me.

So I returned to my church after my small absence and there was another guest preacher present. This was different in that this preacher was a woman, and she was not a stranger, she was from the congregation. She was a good orator, and as she got into her sermon, I was elated. She was preaching about something that I read. I could actually listen with knowledge and understanding instead of just emotion. My knowledge of this particular biblical event would force me to make one of the biggest decisions I have ever made in my life. As the woman's sermon progressed, I heard her mention things incorrectly. I sat there astonished. I looked around to see if anyone else noticed. No one else seemed to notice. In fact, I heard shouts of "GLORY" and "AMEN" louder and louder. I became more and more troubled as it appeared that she was more interested in making a personal statement about her disdain of Solomon's many wives. She was so focused on that aspect that she mentioned things concerning the story incorrectly and out of context. It almost appeared as if she was making a personal statement about someone in the congregation. As the sermon progressed, I looked for anyone in the congregation who knew that this was out of order. I looked left, then right but no takers. I looked up in the balcony and still no takers. Then I looked in front me, as the head preacher sat in his seat attempting to maintain his composure. I looked directly in his eyes, and he knew! He knew that she was preaching this sermon wrong and he did not stop her, nor did he interject at all. I decided that day, that I could not go to a place where the shepherd would stand by and allow his sheep to be misled. That was my last day in the church that I once called home.

THE LITTLE OLD MAN

I now found myself at home with no place to call home, as far as church goes. So being the notorious channel flipper that I am, I was flipping thru the channels and ran across a television program talking about the bible. It was interesting because the focus was not about emotional displays of affection toward The Most High, but observance in the correct fashion. I was mesmerized; in fact, I don't think I blinked until it was over. This little television show on a public access channel led me to the most influential figure of my life. He was a little old man with a full gray beard. He seemed frail until he began to speak. His voice commanded attention, and his wisdom kept you listening. He had been teaching for over three decades when I met him.

You could hear the revolutionary in him as he spoke, being an ex-black panther, but on the flip side you could hear the love for mankind in general as he was also an ex-member of the famous Wings Over Jordan Choir. So needless to say, he was very well rounded. His knowledge about secular and biblical history was astounding. His name was Yachov Ben Yisrael and I consider myself blessed to have been his student.

He was not the teacher for everyone though, and he would be the first to admit that. He was not politically correct at all and I loved it. He was hard on me at times and I even grew to appreciate that, especially after he passed.

One day he passed by me at the television studio where I had volunteered to help with cameras and cleanup. He walked by me and said, "Come on". I said, "Come on where"? He said, "To do the show". The show was a live question and answer biblical show called "As It Is Written". I was absolutely horrified, but I grabbed a bible and went. It would be awesome if I told you it went wonderfully and I was inspired and my life was forever changed, but that's not what happened. I stunk! I didn't know what to stay, I forgot any and all biblical references and as I kept trying to throw the conversation back to him, he sat there quiet and let me sink. I could not believe he asked me to go on a show, only to let me drown on live television. The old man was a genius though. I stunk so bad that now I wanted to go back on to redeem myself. I asked to go back on the show, but he wouldn't let me. I showed up week after week hoping he would ask me again but he wouldn't. Each and every week I was preparing more and more for what I really never wanted to do in the first place. He finally walked past me one day and said "You ready"? I told him, "Yes", and the rest was history.

I was eventually given the position as lead coordinator for the Audio Visual department by Elder Yachov. We began doing television programs together on a regular basis, but then, just as I got comfortable, the old man pushed me on a higher level. We would be scheduled to record a show together, and at the last minute, he wouldn't show up. I would call him and he would say, "I will be there", but he would not arrive. I was upset and confused. This tactic reached its pinnacle when I put together a black history program for the congregation which included a live question and answer session with the Elder at the end. The closer we got to the end of the program, the more I panicked. I called him and he said once again, I will be there, but of course, he never showed, so I had to do his segment. During the next Sermon he stated "Sometimes people do programs and get upset because I don't show up, but I was there, I was there because you were there".

I finally understood what he was doing. He made me grow up. He removed all other people from appearing on shows except a select few and told me that I would be the voice and the face of the congregation. What's funny is I should have seen all of this coming a mile away, because the first time I saw him teach, I went home and said, "I know what I am going to be like when I get old."

FINDING MYSELF
IN THE BOOK

My mentor challenged me from day one. He asked me if I knew who I was and if I could find myself in the bible. No one had ever asked me anything like that. I was stumped of course, because not only could I not find myself in the bible, I couldn't find any of my people in the bible. He asked me if I ever thought it was strange that all the people of the bible were all portrayed to be white in 99% of all movies and literature. This was an interesting statement because most people will tell you that it doesn't matter what color Christ is, but in all the depictions that I had ever seen, he was always white. So the conclusion became, it doesn't matter, as long as he is white. I later found out that the image of Christ that I used to see in my head when I prayed was actually a regular man who posed for a picture, and all the later variations were based off of him. After being directed to a few verses I realized that this image did not fit what was written so I tried to take it out of my mind but I couldn't. Eventually I became free of this image by opening my eyes when I prayed, and the image left my mind. After that experience I understood the commandment, thou shall not make any graven images.

DOES IT REALLY MATTER?

Some will obviously ask the question, does it even matter? We have to consider that the bible is a best seller year after year. The one book that is in almost every household, whether rich or poor, black or white, is the bible. It is estimated that 92 percent of American households have at least one bible. There are 100 million bibles sold every year! With those kinds of numbers, can we afford to say that certain depictions are not accurate but it really doesn't matter? We have to consider what the bible is to those who live their lives by it. It helps direct the upbringing of their kids and assists adult individuals in maintaining healthy relationships, just to say the least. With all this at stake, any erroneous applications of the concepts inside of it must be visited.

Let's consider if there was a text book distributed to 92 percent of all schools and certain depictions were inaccurate, would it matter to you? Would we be ok with our kids learning those concepts? Many people of color were elated when Barak Obama was elected as the first black president of The United States of America. Imagine if a book was written to acknowledge and document his achievement, but the image shown to be him, resembled George Bush. How would that make you feel? Most of us have come in contact with the Rebel Confederate flag. Many of the people that fly the confederate flag state that it is about their heritage not hate. So do you think it would matter to them if Robert E Lee, the confederate war general and hero to many, was depicted in a text book looking like Bill Cosby? If flying their flag is about heritage, why would they allow someone of another ethnic background to take credit for events that they deem historic and honorable? And the answer is, they would not. So if they wouldn't, why would you?

There is an entirely different aspect to the question of why does it matter. Consider how many African-American youth who have grown up reading the bible and was told that it includes God's plan for man. This same bible details the origin of man in general, yet every depiction of the characters in the stories resemble only one group of people. If it includes the origin of man, then every ethnic group should be represented. We must examine what it does to the psyche of African-American youth who have been told that the bible is the key, but can't find any representation, nor has heard any teachings of anyone who looks like them. This problem cannot be ignored or minimized as we have a growing amount of African-Americans who are bleaching their skin to appear more acceptable. We know that Hollywood surely has its share of the blame when it comes to how African-Americans are depicted on the big screen, but we must consider the effect on one's self esteem to grow up believing that there is nothing in heaven or earth that is good that resembles you.

Let us also bring into this conversation that there are increased numbers of African American actors and singers who have undergone plastic surgery to alter their appearance. One of the most successful musicians of all time, Michael Jackson, seemed to be uncomfortable in his own skin. We watched album after album as his nose became smaller and smaller and his skin became lighter and lighter, until he became white. The official story was that he had vitiligo, which is an ailment that causes light spots in your skin. The problem with that is his whiteness was evenly spread across his body. At that time we had never even heard of skin brightening products. Now there are many of these products made specifically for people of color to bleach themselves. We also must remember that Michael Jackson was a Jehovah's Witness as a child. You have to wonder if this low self esteem about his skin color actually began when reading all of his religion's literature, and everyone that was good in the bible was depicted as being a Caucasian. The desire to be white was so strong that he adopted Caucasian children and presented them as his own biological offspring. It is clear to see that biracial children are not born without the traces of both ethnicities. So not only was he transforming himself, but he was transforming his entire so-called offspring and lineage from black to white. How could someone who was worshipped by millions have such low self esteem about themselves?

In 2010 CNN performed a study based on the 1940's white doll vs. black doll test. Most people would like to believe that much has changed but the CNN study found otherwise. When white children were asked about acceptable facial features they overwhelmingly picked white features as being more attractive. When they were prompted to find the ugly person, the white children overwhelmingly picked the dark colored pictures. When they were prompted to find the bad child and the mean child, they always overwhelmingly picked the dark colored children. They called it white bias, and the majority of white children automatically believed they and their features were more acceptable. This is where the 2010 study gets interesting. When black kids were asked the same questions, it was found that the black kids also had white bias. That is amazing! Black people picked the darker colored images as bad, ugly, dumb and mean. Now you have to ask yourself, how did these kids get programmed this way at such an early age? This programming directly plays into the whole skin bleaching epidemic because there were different shades of black children. The lighter shades of black children were found to be more attractive, smart and good by both the white kids and the black kids. So at an early age, American kids somehow derived the conclusion that the darker you are, the more evil you are. If you don't believe that this concept has invaded Christian doctrine, consider the following films and character representations. In Jesus Christ Superstar in the 1970's, the role of Jesus was played by a Caucasian man while the role of Judas was played by a black man named Carl Anderson. Anderson replaced the original actor who was sidelined because of illness. That actor was a black man named Ben Vereen. So you see, Judas was going to be portrayed by a black man one way or the other. In the History channel mini-series "The Bible", which was watched by more than 10 million people each time it aired, Jesus was played by a white man while the devil was played by a black man who looked like Barak Obama. Countless biblical writings from various church organizations present good and evil in the same way, which is black vs white. This constant character representation reinforces the mindset that anything good is white, while everything black is bad. African Americans must educate themselves and their kids on this topic or they may be helping to lower the self-esteem of their children unknowingly, just by going to church! We are constantly inundated with the phrases black Monday, blackmail, black sheep, black magic etc, etc. These sayings help reinforce the idea that black is bad, so good must be white. But how did it get this way?

THE RENAISSANCE PERIOD

The concept is pretty simple. Many of us remember when Sadam Hussein was over thrown as the leader of Iraq. During the celebration of his demise, the statues and images of him were destroyed. The process of destroying someone goes in two forms. There is the physical destruction and there is the mental destruction. The mental destruction is where the remembrance is removed from the minds of people. To perform this, the images of that individual must be removed or altered.

After the period called the dark ages, the period known as the renaissance was born. In this period, all influential characters of any kind were portrayed as being Caucasians. Popes and influential leaders commissioned painting of themselves and Christ. Of course, automatically, Christ was portrayed to look just like them. This period of time was magnified by newly created printing presses. These new presses allowed for mass production of materials that would have been done by hand in times past. It was sort of like their version of the internet. All of a sudden, what was only known in one town, could now be spread to many towns in an expedited manner.

It is also important to note that during this period known as the dark ages, Europe was being controlled by black people who were called Moors. Every year Spain has an event that is called "Running with the Bulls". In this mass event, the Spaniards are running in front of and alongside of the bulls. It is a very dangerous event and many are gored by the horns of the bulls, but the event never stops. It is reported that this event commemorates the overthrowing and the expulsion of the black Moors, or bulls, from their country. Immediately following the expulsion of the Moors, the Spanish, Portuguese, and Dutch spearheaded what came to be known as the trans-

Atlantic Slave Trade. These events are directly related but are rarely even discussed in schools.

So that we may understand that it is a normal thing for Europeans to take the likeness of influential characters and paint them as themselves, we need only look into the Apocrypha. The Apocrypha was originally contained in the 1611 edition of the bible. After some time, these books were removed. There are several reasons for this removal. The 1st & 2nd Maccabees fits into the period after Malachi and before Matthew in the bible. The 1st and 2nd Maccabees detail how Europeans invaded the Holy City of Jerusalem, killed many Jews, sacrificed unclean pigs on Holy altars, and murdered people who continued to observe the Sabbath day. From the beginning, the Euro-Gentiles did not like the Sabbath day and were hell bent on destroying it. Examine what was written in the 1st King James bible as documentation of the deeds that were done in Jerusalem.

> **2 Maccabees 5v25** (Antiochus) "Who comming to Ierusalem, and pretending peace, did forbeare till the holy day of the

Sabbath, when taking the Iewes keeping holy day, hee commanded his men to arme themselues.

v26 And so hee slewe all them that were gone to the celebrating of the Sabbath, and running through the city with weapons, slewe great multitudes".

Also it is written in various other places, in great detail about the destruction caused in Jerusalem by the gentiles. **2 Maccabees 6v4** says "...For the Temple was filled with riot and revelling, by the Gentiles, who dallied with harlots, and had to do with women within the circuit of the holy places, and besides that, brought in things that were not lawfull.

v5 The Altar also was filled with profane things, which the Law forbiddeth.

v6 Neither was it lawfull for a man to keepe Sabbath dayes, or ancient Feasts, or to professe himselfe at all to be a Iewe *(Jew)*".

To this day there is a large debate about the validity of the Sabbath day in Christianity, yet many have no idea that this fight to remove or change the Sabbath day was even before Christ was present on the earth. We must also understand that when Constantine made Christianity the legal religion of the so-called Holy Roman Empire, he changed the Sabbath day from Saturday to Sunday! This took place over 300 years after the birth, death, and resurrection of Christ. Constantine was also not a member or an authoritative figure in the church, so this change was in no way authorized by the church. There is another interesting point to expound upon out of the 1st King James bible as well. This verse details how the invading Euro-Gentiles sought to input images of themselves into the holy Bible, even before Christ.

> **1 Maccabees 3v48** "And laide open the booke of the Law, wherein ye heathen had sought to paint the likenesse of their images".

This explains how we know have bibles that show every individual, regardless of the ethnic background of that individual, as being a Caucasian.

THE N WORD

Let's address the 400 lb gorilla in the room. The so-called n word has polarized the black community. You have people who have no problem with it, some who absolutely abhor it, and then you have those that only have a problem when non-black people use it. So let's go ahead and get it out the way... Nigger, nigger, nigger, nigger!

Now that most of you are terribly horrified, let me show you how the N word appears in the Holy Bible. The most common mistake that most people make when reading the bible is accepting everything that is read for face value. What we have to understand is that the bible was translated. So when examining the intent of a particular verse or phrase it may become necessary to find the original word used in that portion of the writing. When we find that word, it becomes necessary to exercise Etymology, or the history and definition of a particular word so that we may ascertain what context the writer used that particular word.

Now let's get back to the N word. Let's read a verse from the New Testament book of Acts. Acts Chapter 13 verse 1 says "…Now there were in the church that was at Antioch certain prophets and teachers; as Barnabas, and Simeon that was called Niger, and Lucius of Cyrene, and Manaen, which had been brought up with Herod the tetrarch, and Saul. Let's examine Simeon, who was called Niger. First things first, most people will tell you that this word is pronounced Niger with I sound being the more dominant sound. Let's examine this word to see if that is true. The New Testament book of Acts was written in Greek. When we check the Strong's bible dictionary it states this. **Niger (G3526) Pronounced (*neeg'-er).**

Did you notice that this word is pronounced with the e sound not the I sound? So this is in fact the exact word that horrifies most African

Americans to this day. Let's go one step further. The definition says...Of Latin origin; *black*; *Niger*, a Christian: - Niger. So let's recap, Niger pronounced Neeger, is a Latin word and it means black.

If this word was deemed to be offensive during that time, do you think Simeon would have allowed them to call him Neeger?

I recently watched a television program in which a prominent pastor was detailing his disdain for the N word. It was clear to me that he did not understand the etymology of that word. But that's just it, it was only clear to me in my living room. The people in his presence cheered him on, and why not. Today people have adopted the notion that the more people one can get to follow him, the more right he is.

Take a minute to consider what you have just learned. You have learned that a man called Simeon, named after one of the twelve sons of Jacob, was of the prophets and teachers of the word, and he was black. Why is this tid-bit of information an accomplishment in your learning you may ask? Well first ask yourself have you ever heard or seen anything like this in any biblical movie or documentary. Now consider the enormous amount of attention that Hollywood movie makers put into understanding and developing their story line. Consider that the first time any of us found out that there was a weapon that could look thru walls with infrared technology; it was an Arnold Schwarzenegger film. Now with all of the resources available to them, do you believe that Hollywood missed this? It's time that we consider that it was always known. It is also about time that we consider that it must have been Blacked Out.

CURSED BLACK

We are now at the point to discuss the not so secret notion that black people must have been cursed with black skin. This erroneous doctrine was held by slave masters, as it gave excuse for slavery and its cruel measures. After all, if God was mad at those people, you can do anything to them and it's okay. When we examine the feeling of being justified to commit certain acts it gives us the ability to perform some god awful deeds and never lose sleep about it. The average person does not believe that killing someone is a normal thing, but take that same person and put their child in danger and watch them kill without thinking about it. What was the difference? Justification! The person felt justified by the normal nature to protect their family. So if you can make an individual feel justified in their actions, the most god awful deeds now become normal, or maybe even something to be praised. Consider what is written in America's official declaration documents. It is written that all men are created equal. This is what was written at the same time that white men owned slaves because they didn't see black men as men. This mindset sheds more light as to why you hear a grown man referred to as "boy".

Although the Mormon Church did not create this doctrine of blacks being cursed black, no other church took a hold of this doctrine like the Mormons. The Mormons held an openly racist view of African Americans and anyone the like for almost 150 years. Their leaders taught that before men came to this world there was a war between the spirit beings. Long story made short, the spirit beings who were less valiant came to earth cursed with black skin. For this reason, the Mormon church's official doctrine was that no person of color could hold the office of priesthood in their organization. Some of their leaders actually taught that black people were created so that Lucifer will have a presence on the earth.

THE MARK OF CAIN

To further explain the cursed black doctrine we have to examine the faulty principles on which it was derived. The first is that black people are descendants of Cain and that the mark of Cain mentioned in the bible was to be punished with black skin. Let's examine what is written concerning the mark of Cain. Genesis Chapter 4v13 says "...And Cain said unto the (YHWH) LORD, My punishment *is* greater than I can bear.

> Behold, thou hast driven me out this day from the face of the earth; and from thy face shall I be hid; and I shall be a fugitive and a vagabond in the earth; and it shall come to pass, *that* every one that findeth me shall slay me.

And the (YHWH)LORD said unto him, Therefore whosoever slayeth Cain, vengeance shall be taken on him sevenfold. And the (YHWH)LORD set a mark upon Cain, lest any finding him should kill him".

As we see, the mark of Cain was pronounced judgment for any individuals who would kill him. According to what is written, the mark had nothing to do with physical appearance, but more about judgment to anyone seeking their own vengeance. This is an interesting concept considering the fact that many African Americans were killed during the slavery era and many are being killed by the police today. If there was a Mark of Cain that existed in such form, the punishment for slaying us would be severe. What we have noticed is the exact opposite of righteous judgment here in America. During the slavery era, a slave master or the people that worked for him could not be brought up on charges for murder because the slave was his property. The overseer or the officer, inflicted the punishment proposed by the slave master and was thus protected by policy. Examine today's policy. The overseer, or the officer, is allowed to shoot unarmed black men without the possibility of punishment. If there was a so-called Mark of Cain upon black people, it has completely failed us, seeing no judgment, punishment or any type of affliction has happened to the murderers of black people here in this country.

THE CURSE OF HAM

The next erroneous doctrine we must examine is the belief that black people were cursed black through the curse of Ham. When we examine what is written in the bible, we find that it was not actually Ham that was cursed in the first place.

> Genesis Chapter 9v22 says… "And Ham, the father of Canaan, saw the nakedness of his father, and told his two brethren without. And Shem and Japheth took a garment, and laid *it* upon both their shoulders, and went backward, and covered the nakedness of their father; and their faces *were* backward, and they saw not their father's nakedness.
>
> And Noah awoke from his wine, and knew what his younger son had done unto him.

And he said, Cursed *be* Canaan; a servant of servants shall he be unto his brethren".

Canaan was Ham's son, so in actuality it was Ham's son that was cursed, not Ham. Also, if we pay close attention we find that the curse was to be a servant of servants. In other words, the curse had nothing to do with how he looked. In fact, when we examine the bible writings, we find that Ham was already black and could not possibly have been cursed black. This notion comes from the mormon doctrine that all the good spirits were white and thus pure.

Let's examine what is written in the Holy Bible concerning Noah and his three sons. Genesis Chapter 6:10 says "...And Noah begat three sons, Shem, Ham, and Japheth. The Bible clearly states that the earth was overspread with the descendants of these three men. The bible also clearly details the genealogy of these three men. Before we take an in depth look at the genealogy of Ham, let's look at the name Ham and the meaning of it.

Ham as defined in the Strong's Biblical dictionary is defined as (H2526) Hot or burnt. Genesis Chapter 10v6 says "...and the sons of

Ham were Cush, Mizraim, Phut, and Canaan". When we examine the rest of these names in biblical dictionaries, we find that Cush is the Ethiopians, Mizraim is upper and lower Egypt, and Canaan was their brother. Ham signifies burnt or black; and this name was significant of the regions allotted to his family. To the Cushites, or descendants of Cush, were allotted the hot southern regions of Asia, along the shores of the Persian Gulf, to the sons of Canaan, Palestine and Syria; to the sons of Mizraim, Egypt and Libya, in Africa. In conclusion, Ham, which means burnt, denotes the people whom we now call Africans. It is known that the Garden of Eden is located in Africa. This makes sense as melanin, which is only in skin of color, absorbs the harmful rays of the sun naturally. Skin without melanin or color will not do this naturally or without artificial additives.

If we completely digest the information just listed, it dispels several doctrines all at once. I don't think people consider that Israel was called Canaan land before, and it was people that we know as Africans who inhabited that land before it was given to Israel. This concept is enormously important and we will explore it later.

COLOR SPECTRUM

After discussing such an ignorant belief that someone could be cursed black, let's examine some things scientifically to further examine the fallacy of the doctrine that the Mormon Church publicly held, practiced and defended for over 150 years.

> Genesis Chapter 2v7 says... "Yahweh God (YHWH ELOHIM) formed man from the dust of the ground, and breathed into his nostrils the breath of life; and man became a living soul". (World English Bible w/Apocrypha)

This man was obviously a building block for all mankind as the rest of earthly men derived from this creation of the first man. The question then becomes, what did this man look like? There is no one on earth old enough to testify so how would anyone be able to confidently say? Every bible, television show or documentary depicts all these individuals as white or Caucasian. It is very possible that the many depictions of an all white beginning help spawn the erroneous cursed black doctrine in the first place.

Let's see if science agrees with an all white beginning concerning the creation of man. As stated in Genesis Chapter 2v7," man was formed from the dust of the ground". Let us now take a mental picture of what dirt looks like. We find that there are different types of dirt, so the dirt that man was created from must be able to produce all shades of man. The most obvious dirt to be considered is what we call potting soil. Potting soil is the richest of all soil and is midnight black in color. The obvious question then becomes can midnight black produce every other color, including white?

When we examine the color spectrum chart, we find that red, blue, and yellow are primary colors. Other colors are created as these colors are combined in various amounts. When we examine the full color spectrum we find white on one end of the color spectrum chart and black on the other. Does this then prove the all white beginning with white being on one end and black being on the other end?

Like all things in mathematics, for your equation to be proven, you can reverse the process and arrive at the beginning. When we blend all the colors together we get black. So if we were going to start with a color as a building block, it must be a color that can produce every other color. When we visit a hardware store to purchase paint we find that there is a base color and other colors are added to it in order to give us the color that we desire. The end result changes the more colors that are added. So we see that when white is mixed with any other color, it becomes or is taken over by that color. When we perform the same test with black we find the opposite is true. When black is mixed with any other color, all other colors become black and the black remains. So in conclusion, black can create every color in the spectrum, including white, while white on the other hand, can only produce white. So if white was the color of the building block, the entire world would be populated with only white people.

It makes sense then that if you wanted to create a building block that could create all other colors, the first thing created must be a rich deep color that would ultimately be able to produce other colors. The next question to be asked is does this little scientific experiment hold true for physical men, and the answer is yes. Two black people can produce a white child. Today they are called albinos. They are born with white skin, blond hair and light colored eyes. The opposite is not true concerning white. Two white people will not be able to produce a black child. White is a pure color, meaning it is empty of any other colors. That being said, it can only produce the same color. So science agrees that an all white earthly beginning is not possible. It is also interesting to note that recently there was a story in the news about a set of biracial twins. One twin was born with black features, while the other was born with white features. They of course looked alike but were different in color. This would throw some people off because although it is extremely rare, black does have the ability to produce white.

With that being said we must pay particular attention to what was written in the beginning. Genesis 1v26 says "…God said, Let's make man in our image, after our likeness". The man that was created resembles the likeness of God in heaven. Revelation Chapter 4v2-3 says "…Immediately I was in the Spirit. Behold, there was a throne set in heaven, and one sitting on the throne that looked like a jasper stone and a sardius". The jasper and sardius stones are reddish and brownish stones. So he that sat on the throne was a deep brownish red color. Revelation chapter 1 and verse 15 gives more information about this entity in heaven. This entity in heaven described as Alpha and Omega by name, and described in the physical sense as having feet that were like burnished brass, as if they had been refined in a furnace. So the entity that sat upon the throne in heaven definitely speaks against an all white beginning for mankind. As it is written, "let it be done on earth as it is in heaven". It is clear that Hollywood has no intention of telling this story accurately.

THE APOSTLE PAUL

The Apostle Paul of the New Testament is by far one of the most important figures of the New Testament. His writings make up the majority of the New Testament. He was the apostle who was directly sent to the gentiles. This would make him of extreme importance to bible enthusiasts. When dealing with the Apostle Paul we come in contact with several interesting concepts. One is nationality while the other is ethnicity. The two of these are not necessarily the same thing. It is well documented of the sufferings that befell the Apostle Paul as he spread the gospel. In one of these incidents Paul was sentenced to be beaten. He then asked the centurion Acts 22v25 "...Paul said unto the centurion that stood by, Is it lawful for you to scourge a man that is a

Roman. We can clearly see that Paul said that he was a Roman. So when we see depictions of him being a Caucasian we should easily accept that right? Actually we should not. What Paul gave us was his nationality, not his ethnicity. These two classifications are not referring to the same thing. A person's nationality describes the nation that they are legally a citizen of. A person's ethnicity describes the ethnic group to whom a person belongs. If a person of China moves to America and gains citizenship, he is an American by nationality, but his ethnic background remains of China. Paul was mentioning his citizenship as it gave him certain protections under the law. This is confirmed in the next verse. Act 22v26 says... When the centurion heard *that,* he went and told the chief captain, saying, Take heed what thou doest: for this man is a Roman". There was then disbelief that he was actually a Roman. The chief captain then comes to inquire about his nationality. Act 22v27 says "...Then the chief captain came, and said unto him, Tell me, art thou a Roman"? He said, "Yea". The centurion then explained to Paul how costly it was for him to obtain Roman citizenship. Act 22v28 says "...And the chief captain answered, With a great sum obtained I this freedom". And Paul said, "But I was *free* born". Paul was most likely born in a province controlled by Rome so he obtained citizenship as a Roman, just as children of immigrants who are born on U.S. soil are U.S. citizens, even if their parents are not. What is interesting here is the soldiers did not readily believe he was a Roman by his appearance. So the question then becomes, what did he look like? As we back up a chapter we can see what they really thought about Paul. Act 21v37-38 says "...And as Paul was to be led into the castle, he said unto the chief captain, May I speak unto thee? Who said, Canst thou speak Greek? Art not thou that Egyptian"? This is enormous! Paul is accused of being an Egyptian, not a Roman. We must understand that ancient Egyptians were people of color. In fact when we back track to the information given earlier, we find that Egyptians are descendants of Ham, which means burnt. So the soldiers mistook the Apostle Paul for being an African. When we examine the statements made about his ethnicity we find them to be quite different and detailed. In 2 Corinthians 11v22, he says "...Are they Hebrews? so am I, Are they Israelites? so am I". He also says in Romans 11v1 "...I say then, Hath God cast away his people? God forbid. For I also am an Israelite, of the seed of Abraham, *of* the tribe of Benjamin". So in conclusion, his citizenship was of Rome, while his ethnic background was that of a Hebrew. He, being a Hebrew by his own admission, and yet being mistaken for an ancient Egyptian, who were people of color, moves us to the obvious conclusion that the ancient Hebrews were also people of color.

THE MAN WHO IS CALLED JESUS

Hands down, the most important figure of Christianity is the messiah, or Christ who is called Jesus. With such importance on this entity, you would think that there would have been much research performed on everything involving him. Yet when we read the most widely circulated documentation concerning Christ, we find that a considerable amount of information has been blacked out. The majority of visible images of the figure that we know as Christ look the same way. The manner in which he is constantly depicted is Caucasian in ethnicity, with a beard and long hair down to his shoulders. While the wearing of a beard fits biblical figures of that time, the wearing of long hair does not. Let us examine what is written concerning the beards of men. In Leviticus chapter 21v5 it is written "...neither shall they shave off the corner of their beard". It is also written in Psalms 133v2 says "...ointment ran down upon the beard, even Aaron's beard that went down to the skirts of his garment". The beard was so important to the Hebrew Israelites that they were ashamed not to have one. There was an incident where two of King David's servants had their beards cut off by an adversary of Israel. It is written in 2 Samuel chapter 10v5 that "the men were greatly ashamed; and the king said tarry at Jericho until your beards be grown, and then return". The beard was so important that these men were relieved of their duties because their beards had been shaven off. So it is clear that beards would and should be common to all Israelites, but what about long hair? The Apostle Paul stated something in 1 Corinthians that makes it very unlikely that the Messiah had long hair. 1 Corinthians chapter 11v14 says "...does not nature even teach you, that if a man has long hair, it is a shame unto him". Now it is very unlikely that the Apostle Paul would have said that it is a shame for a man to have long hair, if the leader of his faith had long flowing hair down past his shoulders. There is one instance in scripture where a man could have long hair and not be disgraced. This instance was called a Nazarite vow. The details of a Nazarite vow are written in Numbers chapter 6. Numbers chapter 6v3 says "...he shall separate himself from strong drink, and he shall drink no vinegar of wine, or vinegar of strong drink, neither shall he drink any liquor of grapes, nor eat moist grapes or dried". It is written in the next verse that he must not allow any razor to come near his head until the time of his vow is complete. When we examine what was done during the Passover, Christ clearly drank wine, so he was not under any Nazarite vow during that time.

Now that we have addressed the beard and long hair, let us address his ethnicity. In Romans Chapter 9v3-5 it is written "...Christ, my brethren, my kinsmen according to the flesh, who are Israelites, and of whom as concerning the flesh, Christ came". So the apostle Paul clearly states that he is an Israelite and that Christ is an Israelite as well. Let us remember from the former reading that Paul was mistaken for an ancient Egyptian, who were people of color, and he states that Christ was of the same ethnicity as he was. In fact, in Matthew chapter 2v13 it says "...take the young child (Christ) and flee into Egypt". So, just as Paul was mistaken for an Egyptian, Christ was hid amongst the Egyptians. If Christ was a Caucasian he would not have been able to blend in with Egyptians of Africa. In order to get an accurate picture in our mind we must not confuse the people who are in Egypt in present times as the ancient Egyptians. The people who inhabit the land of Egypt in present times are Egyptians by nationality, but are not Egyptians by ethnicity. When we examine the depictions of Egyptians on the pyramids, we clearly see that they were people of color. In fact, when we examine the lineages written in Genesis chapter 10, Egyptians are descendants of Ham, which means burnt or hot, and is the same people who are erroneously said to have been cursed black. The beauty of this is, how could a Caucasian

Christ hide amongst people who were said to have been cursed black? And the answer is, he could not, he would have had to look like them, to hide among them.

THE POWER OF A
NAME CHANGE

Name and facial recognition is how we determine nowadays if we really know someone. Today, if you show someone an image of Jesus, the majority of people will visually recognize him as such, and verbalize his name as being Jesus. The amazing thing is…, we accept an image of an individual who lived during a time where there were no cameras. What is even more amazing is that the image we accept does not match what is written in the bible concerning the people from whom he was derived. How did we come to this?

People are creatures of habit, so we process things according to the number of times we have encountered it. Let's say we hear from five people that a friend of ours, who was the nicest person we knew, but the rumor was that he robbed a bank. The first time we heard it, we might not believe it, but after repeatedly hearing the same thing, we begin to give it validity based on the number of times we have heard it. In actuality, we could have just heard the account of five liars who have agreed to agree on a fictitious account of a situation. This same scenario has sent many innocent people to prison for the rest of their lives.

We have heard so many people testify as to the power that is in the name Jesus, so why would we have reason to question his name? Once again, some will ask, why does it matter? Consider what is written in the New Testament book of Acts chapter 4v12. It reads "...for there is none other name under heaven given among men, by which we must be saved". According to what is written here, the name appears to be important. Since it does appear to be of most importance, we must investigate the name, as salvation depends on it. If we forensically investigate the name as we would a murder case, we must have a timeline of events that either exonerates or derives at a particular conclusion.

The current year is 2016, so in investigating the name, its conception should date back 2,016 years. When we examine the name Jesus, we encounter validity issues almost immediately. When we examine the first King James Bible, printed in the year 1611, the name of Jesus is not there. The name that is written in the 1611 version of the King James Bible is "IESUS", (which is pronounces ee-A-zeus). Upon investigation, we find that there was no letter "J" in the English alphabet in the year 1611. This fact alone makes the name Jesus an utter impossibility! If we think back just a few years ago, in one of the most popular movies of all time, the passion of the Christ, there was a scene in which his mother yelled out his name. The name she yelled out was "YAHSHUA". Upon investigation of the name of Yahshua, we find corroborating evidence of its accuracy. YAH, which is GOD's name, as evidenced by Psalms 68v4 "...he is extolled (*or called*) by his name YAH". What you may see in a new bible is "JAH", but please remember, there was no letter "J" in the English language when the first King James Bible was printed. When we scroll through the names of the prophets we find names such as Isai(Yah),

Jeremi(Yah) and so on and so on. This same concept explains why the highest praise is Hallelu(Yah), and it means praise you Yah!

The next step of our investigation of the name leads us to examine the current name that the majority of people use and have accepted as gospel. The obvious question is, why would the powers-that-be change the messiah's name to IESUS, pronounced (ee-A-Zeus), which later came to be known as JESUS. We must first acknowledge the name Zeus contained in this name. Zeus is one of the principal gods of the European pagan gentiles who invaded, conquered, and occupied Yerus-alem, later called Jerusalem, many times over. In the conquering spirit of the heathen, the names of influential figures must be changed to fit their culture. This allows for a later cultural theft, whereby they, the conquering power, can claim that the particular individual in question was of their ethnicity. The ancient Israelites were Hebrews, but the name Jesus is of European decent. This name change is what makes it possible for people to believe that Christ was a Caucasian. We must understand that the ethnicity of a person can be assumed by the names that they carry. For instance, if I stated that my friend Sadam was coming over, would you expect to see a Caucasian or a Middle Eastern person? If I stated that my co-worker Bob was meeting us for dinner, would you be expecting a black man or a white man? This is the power of a name change. The name that one carries is the very first identifier of their cultural identity.

Since the name that one carries is the first identifier of his or her culture, conquering nations have always had a tendency to change the names of influential characters in order to represent them as themselves. Many have heard of the names Shadrach, Meshach, and Abednego. What many of us do not know is that those names are not their original names. These names were giving to them to glorify the pagan god and pagan culture that ruled over them. Their real names were Hanniniyah, Azariyah, and Mishael. These names glorified the God of Israel and the culture of the Israelites. It's ironic that we remember and even cling to the pagan names even though it is clearly stated in the bible that they were given these names by an occupying power. (Daniel 1v6-7) These three were not the only people who had their names changed. Daniel's name was also changed and Joseph's name was changed by Pharaoh in Egypt. This brings to mind the painful account of the character Kunta Kente in the movie Roots. He was repeatedly beaten until he accepted his new Christian name. This name would be an identifier that his culture was dominated and he has accepted the culture of the ruling authority.

The power of a name change is so powerful that it causes people to look at something every day and not recognize it for what it is, all because the name was changed. Millions of people have grown up with a depiction of The Last Supper on their wall. If you ask them about the picture using the name of The Last Supper, they can acknowledge it. On the other hand, if you ask them if they have a picture of Passover, they will reply no. Because the name of the picture is called The Last Supper, millions of people do not recognize this event for what it was, and that Biblical Holy Day is called Passover.

JOSEPH PRINCE OF EGYPT

We must also add into this every growing equation, that the children of Israel lived amongst the Egyptians and eventually were enslaved by them. The most notable figure in the beginning of that era was a man named Joseph. Joseph was disliked by his brothers because of the preferential treatment that he received from their father. Joseph was looked upon in high regards because he was the son of his father's old age and because of his dreams. Joseph, one of the twelve sons of Jacob, was disliked by his brothers because of those dreams. It is even written that as he approached them they stated, "behold this dreamer cometh". His brothers sold him into slavery, but his trials turned into the vehicle for his triumph. He rose from a slave to next in command under Pharaoh King of Egypt. When there was a famine in the land, the children of Israel came into Egypt to buy food, but did not recognize their brother the Hebrew amongst the Egyptians. Joseph was different in name and clothing only. As it is written in Genesis chapter 41v42 that Pharaoh "took off his ring from off his hand, and put it on Joseph's hand, and arrayed him in vestures of fine linen, and put a gold chain about his neck; and made him to ride in the second chariot which he had". These were merely outward upgrades, yet it is written that his brothers did not recognize Joseph as their brother, but saw him as an Egyptian. It is written that Joseph saw his brothers and knew them but made himself strange unto them and spake roughly with them. Genesis chapter 42v8 says "...and Joseph knew his brethren but they knew him not". This now makes the third correlation between the appearance of the Egyptians, the people who descendant from those called burnt face and the ancient Hebrews. This is far too many instances to disregard.

BLACK UPON ME

We must not ignore the psychological effects upon a group of people to see constant references of evil and have it associated with how they look. It has become a constant occurrence to see black people who are accused of a crime shown in an aggressive manner on television. To understand this we must deal with a few basic principles that are common to all people. When two people are engaged in a conversation there is a unspoken of safe zone. This is an area of space that exists between them. If one of them approaches and closes that distance, this gives off an aggressive under tone and the conversation can easily grow into an argument because the safe zone has been violated. This occurs repeatedly on television when black people are accused of a crime. The mug shots of white people are shown with a safe distance between them and the camera. The mug shots of black people are zoomed in enormously. When your brain processes this, it will automatically make this individual appear to be threatening, because their likeness is too close to you. By zooming in on the pictures, the news stations produce the allusion that this individual has entered your safe zone, and you are now forever threatened by this individual, and everyone that resembles them.

We must understand that there are many different shades of black. Even today, we see many Africans who come to America of their own will and have not intermarried with any other group, yet they are not all extremely dark. One of the biggest misconceptions about black people is that we were all one color or shade of black. Most people may not be aware that black people can get darker by being in the sun for a prolonged period, but after that period ends, we get back to our normal shade. This normal shade doesn't change unless there is a prolonged exposure to the sun. In fact, often times it is quite evident which individuals labor in direct sunlight by the shade of their skin. I have had family members and friends who went on vacation and I almost didn't recognize them because they were so dark. When we examine the things written in the scriptures of the Holy Bible, we find several self-designated descriptions of people who describe themselves as black.

In the case of being made blacker by reason of increased exposure to the sun, we find a clear example written in the Song of Solomon. It is so clear in fact, that I have watched several televangelists tell this story and almost re-write the bible to do so. Several words have been altered in many new bibles to substantiate the false claim. Many people think that a bible is a bible, but there are many different versions of the King James Bible itself. By using an Old King James Bible, we can see what was written before the change, and by using a Strong's Concordance and Dictionary, we can see the original word used before the translation. Doing these things in tandem allows us the opportunity to get an accurate understanding without anyone's interpretation.

In Song of Solomon chapter 1v5, the Shulamite girl describes herself as being not only black, but extremely black. This description is so vivid and undeniable that it has caused many to make heartfelt attempts at denying this passage. Song of Solomon Chapter 1v5 says… "I am black, but comely, O ye daughters of Jerusalem, as the tents of Kedar, as the curtains of Solomon". Let us first get a biblical breakdown of the term as the tents of Kedar. Kedar was a descendant of Abraham by way of Ishmael. Kedar in Hebrew (Strong's number H6938) and it means dusky. Next, lets examine the definition for the original word used for black in Song of Solomon chapter 1 verse 5.

The original word used was Shakor, Strong's number H7838. The definition says "...properly *dusky*, but also (absolutely) *jetty:* - black". So not only does the definition say black, but it says jet black like dusk night. Armed with this information I want you to consider how gravely incorrect the current American understanding is of this scripture. I personally witnessed an extremely educated minister with a rather large following, explain to his congregation that this scripture did not refer to how she looked. In fact, the word "black" was changed to "tan" in order to fit what happens to Caucasians after a prolonged period of sunlight exposure. This false belief is exposed even more as you continue reading in Song of Solomon. Song of Solomon chapter 1 v6 says... "Look not upon me, because I *am* black, because the sun hath looked upon me". Here we clearly see that she has gotten darker by reason of the sun, so in fact it is a clear description of her physical appearance. There is even more information yet to mention. As we continue reading, she explains how she has had prolonged exposure to the sun. She states in verse 6 "...my mother's children were angry with me; they made me the keeper of the vineyards". By her own admission, her jet black state has been caused by working outside in the vineyard. As we examine photos of slaves in America, we can quickly tell the difference between the house slaves and the field slaves. The slaves who worked in the fields were always blacker, by reason of the sun. When we take all of this information into account, we begin to understand why the word was changed to tan. Caucasians tan, while blacks get blacker. So it is obvious that this change was done as a deliberate attempt to blackout all involvement of black people in the holy Bible.

WHITE & RUDDY

In the spirit of change, we don't have to go far in the same book to find yet another egregious change in the scripture. This change is actually located in the King James Bible, but thanks to word definition, we never have to except someone's interpretation of what they think this means. In Song of Solomon Chapter 5, the Shulamite girl begins to describe Solomon. Song of Solomon chapter 5v10 says "...My beloved is white and ruddy". It is amazing how the same televangelists that say that black doesn't mean black; never say that white doesn't mean white. After looking into this further, white really doesn't mean white. After performing a word search, we find that the original Hebrew word used for ruddy is Adom (Strong's H122), which means rosy and red. The original Hebrew word used for white is tsakh (Strong's H6703) and it means "dazzling, or sunny, or bright, or (figuratively) *evident: - or* clear, or dry, or plainly, or white". So in examining the possible ways in which this word can be used, white is the last possibility. The first is dazzling and then bright. So what appears to have happened is that "bright" was translated as "white" for obvious reasons. Another interesting note is that if you continue reading the next verse we find that his hair is described as being "bushy locks".

In the Old Testament book of Lamentations chapter 5 there was great mourning over the state of the children of Israel during one of our many captivities. In verse 10 of chapter 5 it is written that "...Our skin was black like an oven because of the terrible famine". The prophet Jeremiah, who is constantly depicted as being Caucasian in any and all movies or pictures, has openly stated how black the children of Israel have gotten because of the malnutrition inflicted upon the ancient Israelite people during the particular captivity or slavery being discussed in this passage.

It is sad that we would have to state the obvious, but no amount of malnutrition would ever cause a white man to turn black!

THE BIBLE, AS IT IS TAUGHT TODAY

The bible as it is taught today is a source of low self-esteem for many people of color. The biblical stories are constantly narrated with the notion that all of its characters are Caucasian in ethnicity. As a result, many people grow up believing that there is no real connection between the bible and people of color. When we actually read the bible as a history book, and take the emotional sensationalism out of it, we find that people of color, particularly descendants of slaves, should feel the deepest connection of any other people. The reasoning behind this is the bible is a historical documentation of GOD's chosen people, the Hebrews. In this historical documentation it is stated over and over again about the many different captivities that the Hebrew people have encountered. That's right; I said the many captivities of the Hebrew people. You see, most of us learn of the bible from someone else's narration, and many of us have heard of the Egyptian captivity. What we did not hear is that the nation of Israel was punished many times by being enslaved by another people. There is a reason for this. The nation of Israel was created to be servants to YHWH. The children of Israel have two options, either serve YHWH or serve your enemies. So one way or another, the children of Israel would constantly be in servitude. Understanding this, the descendants of slaves should feel a deep connection with the Most High, as his form of punishment fits the history of their lives. There are many different scriptures to verify this statement, but one that jumps out at you is the proclamation to Israel from YHWH in Jeremiah chapter 5 and verse 19. It is written "...Like as you have forsaken me and have served strange gods in your land, so shall you serve strangers in a land that is not yours". It becomes necessary after stating this passage to mention that the Old Testament book of Judges is a 430 year period that is riddled with various captivities of the children of Israel. For one reason or another, this history and the propensity of GOD to punish his people through slavery are mysteriously overlooked. If the bible was taught with detail to historical accuracy, maybe people of color would not be so ashamed of slavery. The truth is, most so-called African-Americans are ashamed about slavery and will not discuss it with their kids. But why should a people be ashamed of surviving one of the most horrific human trafficking atrocities of all time? This problem is compounded as those who do tell the story are somehow labeled as racists who won't let go of the past. Meanwhile, year after year we hear different accounts of holocaust survivor stories and none of those people are accused of being racist for telling their history.

DESEGREGATION OR DE-SANCTIFICATION

Desegregation has, for the most part, been regarded as a positive development in the area of equality for so-called African Americans. Segregated in its simplest form means separated. That being said, the post slavery south was segregated, or separated amongst blacks and whites. The real issue of segregation was the deplorable conditions in which services were rendered unto black people during this time. Most black people began to desire the accommodations of their white counterparts. So the obvious answer to the question of unequal services was for blacks to gain access to the same services that whites were given access to. There was however, another answer which was stated over and over during the Civil Rights era. This answer was called 'Separate but Equal'. This option was to allow black people to remain separate from whites, yet have equal services. This option was not desired by America for reasons unclear during that time. Looking in hindsight, the reason for rejecting such an option is now crystal clear. The process of desegregation was a painful one for America. The idea was immediately hated by southern whites, yet promoted by the government. What did the government see that the average white person couldn't? It is now clear why the option of separate but equal was not pushed by the government. This option would have allowed a people once enslaved, to operate, grow, and thrive completely amongst themselves. This option could prove to be disastrous in the future if this separate people began to grow and thrive without America's monitoring. This situation automatically brings to mind the story of the Israelites in ancient Egypt. As the story goes, the children of Israel journeyed into Egypt and lived separate from them. After new leadership gained power in Egypt, it was decreed that this separate people have grown too much. It is stated in Exodus chapter 1v9–10, "the children of Israel are more and mightier than we. Let us deal wisely with them, lest they multiply and when there fall out any war, they join to our enemies".

Most people will say that this correlation is absurd, as America is too strong to be paranoid concerning the doings of its ex-slaves. Well we don't have to look far in America's past to find evidence of such racial paranoia. During World War 2 America imprisoned American citizens of Japanese descent, believing that they may join with their native country and war against America. Many of these people had never been to Japan but were born in America and some even veterans of other wars, but that didn't matter. In 1942 President Roosevelt signed an executive order to relocate all Americans of Japanese ancestry to concentration camps inside of America. These people had done no crime and were citizens, but were locked up none the less.

America's dealing wisely with people of color was to push desegregation forward even though whites hated it. The American government understood the possibilities of having a separate people grow from the inside of their country. There is also a little word play that comes to light as we get deeper into this subject. When we say the word "segregation" most people say that this is bad. Yet if I say the word "sanctified", most people would say that this is a good term. The problem is, these words have the same meaning. Sanctified means separated or set apart as does segregate. So when so-called African Americans were "desegregated", we were also "de-sanctified". Doesn't sound so good when you put it like that does it? We must also note that no other ethnic group in America has ever been desegregated. Every other ethnic group in America tends to live and share commerce amongst their own people. It only makes sense, why would you spread out and divide your power, when you can gather together and magnify your power? This is the reason we have areas that are completely occupied and controlled by specific ethnic groups. These ethnic groups are not attacked when they own and operate stores in these areas. Many people wonder why black people haven't done the same, but we have and they were attacked.

We have a clear example of the terror that occurs when black people become independent from the power system in mass. Tulsa, Oklahoma boasted one of the most successful black communities in America history. Oklahoma was originally set as a black and Indian state as blacks travelled the trail of tears with Native Americans. Because of the terror from white America, the African American and Native Americans were forced to work and trade only amongst themselves. These practices proved profitable for this community. The Greenwood area of Tulsa, Oklahoma boasted over 600 successful black businesses that were created, financed, and operated without white help or intervention. This area was 36 blocks and was called Black Wall Street and Little Africa. The Greenwood area of Tulsa Oklahoma included grocery stores, schools, a bank, a hospital, law offices, libraries and the list goes on. The Black Wall Street area of Tulsa was likened unto a mini Beverly Hills. The envy and retaliation for being successful was fierce from white Americans! All of this great wealth and ingenuity was destroyed in less than 12 hours! America will not acknowledge this state-sponsored mass killing in any fashion. The entire community was burned to the ground. Planes were flown overhead and barrel bombs were dropped on a residential and business district. It was stated by survivors that whites gathered around the outskirts of the city and watched with their kids, the same way they gathered together to watch lynchings of black people. To add insult to injury, Oklahoma solidified the assault by passing a law that stated, if land was burned, it could not be built upon again. In other words, no insurance claims were paid and the community was not rebuilt after whites burned it down. So America learned from leaving blacks alone to grow amongst ourselves without their money and consent. So it has become clear that desegregation was not just about integrating our people, but more about limiting our commerce and ability to survive amongst ourselves. In other words, "Let us deal wisely with this people"

Into Egypt Again

Most people will ask, what does America have to do with Egypt? We have to first understand that the bible was written before America was so-called discovered, so the actual name will not be listed, but the attributes of the nations are described thoroughly. In the Torah, which contains the first five books of the Holy Bible, the book of Deuteronomy details the blessings and the curses of the children of Israel. If the ancient Israelites walked according to the covenant that was given to them then there would be blessings, but if they walked contrary to the culture given unto them then there would be curses. As documented in The Wars of the Jews by the historian Josephus Flavius and various other places, the Europeans invaded

Jerusalem in 70 A.D. and killed over 1.2 million Israelites and sold the remaining to work in the salt mines in Africa. It is necessary to note that the invading Europeans came from the north, so obviously the Israelites who fled, were forced to run further down into Africa to get away from the invading Europeans. One of the phases of the curses began with the invasion from the gentiles. In Deuteronomy chapter 28v68, it is written that YHWH "shall send Israel into Egypt again with ships". To explain this thoroughly we first must understand that it says "again". That being said, anyone who claims to be the descendants of the ancient Israelites must be able to provide a historical account of slavery after the Egyptian captivity. We often hear claims of people asserting that they were a part of the Egyptian captivity, but the blessings and the curses were not given until after the Egyptian captivity was over, so mentioning the captivity before the mandate is a clever trick, but it carries no weight at all. The next part to examine is the portion that describes how the Israelites would get to this new Egypt. The mode of transportation that was mentioned was by way of ships. We have to understand the proximity of physical Egypt and Israel. The ancient Israelites walked into physical Egypt, so in this instance Egypt refers to the bondage and captivity that would be inflicted upon them in the new places that they would enter into by way of ships. We understand that the transatlantic slave trade transported people as cargo all over the world to be sold as slaves. The final point to examine is the similarities between Egypt and the United States of America. When we examine the makeup of America we find that it was designed as an Egyptian replica. There are pyramids all over America. In fact, almost every house is made in the image of a pyramid. Even the church buildings are almost always built with three triangle images and a steeple on top. The steeple is a phallic symbol. A phallic symbol is an image of male genital power and it comes from Egypt. The Washington monument is also a phallic symbol and serves no purpose other than to mimic Egypt. We have to understand the Egyptians built the largest and most successful empire of all time. So it is not a stretch to believe that other kingdoms would attempt to model their kingdom after one of the most powerful kingdoms of all time. There are various places in America that are named after Egypt, such as Memphis and have constructed large pyramids in or around their city skyline. Almost every major city's downtown skyline in America contains a pyramid styled building and a Washington monument styled phallic symbol. If all of this is not enough evidence, just examine the back of the dollar bill. Why would a seemingly Christian country have an image of a pyramid complete with the all seeing eye of Horus, an Egyptian god, on its most circulated denomination of currency?

When we go back to the biblical account of the Israelites in Egypt, we find the governing authority attempting to limit the rate of prosperity among this visiting nation. Exodus chapter 1 v11 says "...they set over them task masters to afflict them in their burdens". This, work them to death tactic was set in order to slow down the growth of the Israelites. The tactic backfired! The more the Israelites were worked, the more they multiplied and grew as a people. Eventually, a more dastardly approach was implemented. Exodus chapter 1 and verse 15 speaks of the official government mandate, which would be called an executive order today, to kill all Israelite male babies as soon as they were born. Why just attack the boys you ask? The answer is that the male carries the seed, meaning the child will be what the father is. As we know in weddings there is a custom that says, who gives this woman away? This marrying woman then begins a life with this man and takes his name. What this truly means is that the women will be absorbed into the culture, as the babies that they produce will be from the seed of the man, which in this case will be from the ruling power, since the number of males from their own ethnic group is greatly diminished.

BLACK-POPULATION CONTROL

When we examine what is happening with black males in America today we find similar tactics being used to slow down the reproduction rate among so-called African Americans. During the time of legalized slavery, black males were a financial asset and commodity. My grandmother, who is 98 years old, was 1 of 19 children in her immediate family and household. In my own family, just check out the drop in reproduction. My grandmother was 1 of 19, she then had 5 children and almost none of her children had more than two children. Changes in mindset gradually increased from generation to generation which produced less offspring as the need for large families declined. Also, during sharecropping, the period immediately following slavery, more males meant more production and thus more money for the entire family. After slavery in America was no more, there then became a necessity to limit the numbers of these people who were once completely controlled by the ruling race of people.

THE CHEATING HUSBAND SYNDROME

Mass incarceration is one of the procedures of population control being used against so-called African Americans. Mass incarceration separates the males from the females and thus effectively erases the possibility of procreation. The prison system as we know it today was invented expressly for this newly freed slave. Prior to slavery, there was no prison industrial complex. The prison system accomplishes a deeply hidden desire of the ruling class of white America, which is the desire to abort any possible uprising. For many white Americans, there is a constant thought of a black uprising. Let me point out that I said many, but not all. Most Caucasians are enjoying their own lives and have no idea that these things are even going on. The wealthy elite or powers-that-be, are in control of this one. The thought of a possible uprising has created a need in the mind of the powers-that-be, to criminalize black people as a whole. Special terms where invented to separate black offences from white offences. Congregating vs. loitering is a clear example of such word usage. It is a legal right for a group of people to "congregate", yet when black people gather together the term "loitering" is used and thus a legal right has been transformed into a criminal offense. During hurricane Katrina, many people were forced to make difficult decisions to stay alive. The manner in which those events were documented made it easy to discern if the individual was Caucasian or African American. When a black person took a boat to get to safety, the words "loot" or "stolen" was used. When Caucasians performed the same action the term "commandeered" was used. In the different word usage you can see how two people performed the same action, yet only one was described as a criminal.

Even though there are many so-called minority groups in America, only the so-called African American is treated in this fashion to this degree. The reason for this is simple and is explained in a concept called Cheating Husband Syndrome. Cheating Husband Syndrome is a process of thought in which the husband who has engaged in infidelity within his marriage, begins to vigorously watch and accuse his wife of cheating. In many cases the wife doesn't even know that her husband has engaged in such activity. None the less, his conscience goes into gear and begins to expect his wife to retaliate in like fashion. All of a sudden the wife begins to notice that every day actions such as getting the mail have all of a sudden turned into a criminal offense. The wife now finds herself being accused of having an affair with the mail man. This accusation has nothing to do with the wife or anything in the wife's heart, but it has everything to do with the past and or present actions of the husband. America's past actions against the African American people have been deplorable. These actions have not been acknowledged or rectified.

Other so-called minority ethnic groups in America don't face this because those groups came to this country of their own will. This so-called African American is the only group of people who were brought to America against their will, and forced to work without pay among other things. Years and years of undiagnosed Cheating Husband Syndrome have developed into a privatized prison system and a domestic policy that encourages and profits from the criminalization of so-called African Americans.

BIOLOGICAL WARFARE

Biological warfare is another effective method of population control. It has been widely discussed and disputed that America has previously used biological warfare on the shores of America. After the Native indigenous people of America were no longer of use to colonial man, a method of extermination was sought for. Some say that this was only a thought and that they didn't carry it out. Others have stated that the tactic was definitely carried out. Either way, it was written down by Lord Jeffrey Amhurst, commanding general of British forces in North America, that it was America's intention to kill the natives with the use of biological weaponry, specifically utilizing small pox infected blankets.

One incident in particular that took place in America and cannot be disputed is the Tuskegee experiment where people of color were told they were receiving free healthcare, while in fact they were being examined as they died from a curable disease. They were lied to and given fake medicine that could never treat them of their condition. In the process of being smiled upon while given false medication, these infected people were passing the infection (syphilis) to their wives and even unborn children. They were also blacklisted from receiving healthcare from any other source. Even when penicillin became widely available, these people were put on a Do-Not-Treat list. So of course, many of them died slow and painful deaths, all authorized by the US government. People often listen to the name of the Tuskegee experiment and automatically believe that it was a project performed by locals of that area. In actuality, the Unites States Public Health Service (USPHS) and the Center for Disease control (CDC) were in charge of this dastardly project. In fact, meetings were held regularly at the CDC to discuss the continuation of this horrible program.

This human science project began with a grant from the Julius Rosenwald fund that was supposedly setup to examine the prevalence of syphilis in the black community and the possibility for mass treatment. Julius Rosenwald was one of the founders of Sears and Roebuck. The Julius Rosenwald Fund went to the United States Public Health Service (USPHS) to get the project started. It is stated that the fund ran out of money in 1929 but the director of USPHS Dr. Talifero Clark suggested continuing the study to examine the decline of health in untreated blacks infected with syphilis. The study was proposed to last from six to nine months, but this evil practice continued for 40 years!

According to a report done by CNN, while the US government was authorizing the Tuskegee experiment, there were other unethical racist experiments happening as well. CNN reported that the United States Public Health Service (USPHS), also conducted similar experiments in prison houses. Research was conducted at a US prison that involved injecting inmates with gonorrhea to study the effects of penicillin. They even went so far as to send in infected prostitutes in the prison, located in Guatemala, to sleep with inmates in order to infect them. Some inmates were given direct inoculations with the syphilis bacteria. Experiments were also said to have been performed in Sing Sing Prison located in New York. Dr. John C. Cutler of the United States Public Health Service participated in the Guatemalan study, the Tuskegee experiment, and in inoculation experiments in the New York prison.

When the events of the Tuskegee experiment were made public, there were automatic connections made with the experiments of Nazi Germany. What is also interesting to note, is the names of the individuals who led the programs. Let us first consider that the Tuskegee experiment began with the Julius Rosenwald fund. He was a Jewish immigrant from Germany. Although I must mention there is no direct listing of any known involvement of him or his fund in any of the experiments. It is also important to note that

Rosenwald funded many schools and YMCA's in black communities. The name and nationality connection with these events are interesting enough to note though. The list of names of a few high up officials involved either directly or indirectly are as follows: Dr. J.R. Heller, Oliver Wenger, Raymond Vonderlehr, and Dr. R.H. Kampmeir just to name a few. If you know anything about names and the countries in which they originated, this list is somewhat interesting. It is also interesting to note that Lord Amherst, who is accused of using biological agents against the Natives of America, was also of German descent.

It is also important to note that most of the individuals who participated in these unethical practices have written books, have colleges and towns named after them, and have raised sons and daughters who grew up to become doctors themselves. I was told about an incident by my mentor Yachov Ben Yisrael concerning a visit to a doctor's office for one of his granddaughters. He said that he sat in the doctor's waiting area constantly looking at the name of the doctor and wondering how he knew that name. He said it finally came to him as he was sitting in the chair directly in front of the doctor. Elder Yachov stated to the doctor, "Your father was one of the doctors involved in the Tuskegee experiments"! He said the doctor's eyes got big but he answered not a word. My elder told me he then picked up his granddaughter and walked out. As usual in American society, the people who do the most harm to people of color are celebrated as heroes in other circles.

VACCINATIONS

So far we have several major scale biological atrocities committed by the highest health organizations in the United States. Regrettably, we are not done. In Tuskegee, Guatemala, and Sing Sing Prison in New York, the Centers for Disease Control (CDC) was directly involved in implementing the biological atrocities that occurred in those areas. In another large scale bio-attack on American soil the CDC is also implicated.

With the desire to kill off the Indians and the letters found documenting the desire, coupled with the small pox breakout within the same period of time, a definite link was established. The powers-that-be have learned from their previous mistakes. By developing vaccines that cause massive medical problems, but take years to culminate, the powers-that-be have introduced for themselves plausible deniability. This is where, even if it is ever proven, they can claim they didn't know it would happen, solely based upon the amount of time the biological agents will take to finally kill their subjects.

Millions of Americans believe that vaccines are completely safe and must be utilized to keep the public safe. In my own experiences I began to wonder why so many people I knew were inflicted with ailments that no one had when I was younger. I grew up in a relatively poor area of Atlanta called Pool Creek. Although many of us had little or no access to healthcare, we were relatively healthy. As I got older I began to run into people who had asthma, allergies, and various skin issues. When I was little all kids played outside. We had no video games, only board games, and board games were things you played when you couldn't go outside. So needless to say, a kid with asthma who couldn't ride his bike for miles and miles and or play street ball all day would have stuck out tremendously. Today's kids don't go outside so those same issues don't apply. Now there are enormous amounts of kids that have various issues. The million dollar question is, where did all these issues come from?

In 1973, Senator Edward Kennedy led a subcommittee to investigate the atrocities of the Tuskegee experiment in order to make sure nothing like that could ever happen again. This resulted in a public law called the National Research Act of 1974 that outlined the specifics on biomedical and behavioral research. It is amazing, the most powerful and advanced country in the world needs a law to tell them not to turn living people into lab rats!

Now the nephew of Senator Kennedy, Robert Kennedy is now leading a fight against the CDC to take toxic ingredients out of the vaccines that are given to American children. I have had my own run-ins dealing with this problem of vaccinations. I never was a person who read for recreation or research, I read to pass whatever test I had to take. So needless to say, when I discovered a conflict in my heart concerning vaccinations, I really had no info on the subject, nor did I get off my John Brown hind parts to do any. My conflict arose when getting one of my children vaccinated, after I began studying the bible. I had basically become an amateur researcher. As I am in the doctor's office there was a pause before the vaccine could be administered. The nurse had to get my signature on a piece of paper. The nurse turned around to see what was taking so long for me to give authorization for my child to be given this shot. She then asked me, "What are you doing"? I replied, "I am reading this before I sign it". She said "Nobody does that". I then realized that my life was beginning to change. I was absolutely horrified by the things that were contained on this vaccination waiver. This waiver said that everything in the world could possibly happen to my innocent child from death to life long illness for which there is no cure. Upon signing the waiver, I would be releasing the doctor's office and vaccine maker from any and all liability. I was absolutely floored. My life was beginning to change, but I didn't feel comfortable enough not to do it, so I signed the waiver and had my child vaccinated. I was one of the lucky ones, no immediate problem arose. Upon doing a tiny bit of research, I now know why the ailments of people I encountered all of a sudden grew.

Robert Kennedy wrote a book called Deadly Immunity and has done countless interviews concerning the deadly amount of poisons contained in vaccines. In respect to him I will relay his message that he is not against vaccines, only against the poisonous agents contained in vaccines. I, on the other hand am completely against them because of the repetitive nature of this country to allow such deeds to be done. In other words, I don't believe any law will stop the powers-that-be. I believe they will find a loop hole and operate in it until such loop hole is discovered. Then a new loop hole will be configured and so on and so on.

The increase in ailments among children appeared to reach epidemic proportions in 1989. According to Robert Kennedy, this happened because Congress passed a law in 1986 that made it illegal to sue any vaccine producer. When I learned this, I immediately thought about the waiver I signed. The biggest problem with the waiver situation was that I was the only one in the office who even read it. All the other parents in the doctor's office signed the waiver without even attempting to investigate what it stated.

After the pharmaceutical companies received diplomatic immunity for the harm that they were about to cause, they of course ran wild. The amount of Vaccines scheduled to be administered suddenly increased from 10 to 24 making the pharmaceutical companies even richer than they already were. One of the major issues with these shots is that they contain high levels of mercury. It is well known and documented that mercury causes the blood cells to sickle, and thus caused sickle cell anemia. This ailment affected mostly black people. Where did this mercury come from you ask, you guessed it, the vaccines? High mercury is connected to autism, SIDS, ADHD, a form of terets, OCD, asthma, food allergies, bipolar disorders, diabetes, etc., etc. Mercury can alter your hormones and destroy your immune system. All of these ailments have dramatically increased since 1989. We all have heard how poisonous lead is to our children, yet mercury, which is a 1000 times more neurotoxin than lead, is given to children in the form of a vaccination every day.

Today many clinics are advertising flu shots. Many of the flu shots contain thimerosal which is a deadly form of mercury. According to Robert Kennedy Jr., the vaccines with high levels of mercury consistently find themselves in the black community. He also states that black boys have a 250% greater chance of being affected by higher doses of mercury than any other group. In other words, it was designed to kill African American men before they become men. Remember the cry in Egypt, if it is a male child, kill it, if it is a girl keep it alive.

Dr. William Thompson, a senior level official for the CDC blew the whistle about a 2004 CDC study about the effects of vaccines on black boys in particular. He and other officials were instructed by CDC to lie about the findings and the data thrown away. These facts were stated before Congress by Senator Bill Posey. The numbers are absolutely alarming. Robert Kennedy stated over 100,000 black boys have become autistic since this information has been known by the public, as the powers-that-be, always knew!

VACCINES & THE HIV/AIDS CONNECTION

Many have heard the old adage about Hiv/Aids deriving from a monkey virus that may have entered an African hunter thru a scratch of some sort and was then transmitted to the human population. What is conveniently left out of those discussions is that the same company that develops vaccines also happens to be the manufacturer of biological weaponry for the U.S. government. So to put this in perspective, the same company that is charged with preserving life also has a contract to destroy life. That sounds like contracting the fox to guard the hen house!

The Royal Society of London's conference on the origin of HIV/AIDS concluded that it is highly probable that HIV/AIDS derived from contaminated vaccines given mostly to people of African descent. We must understand how the chimpanzees and monkeys get involved in the scenario. The monkeys and chimpanzees were used to make the vaccines. When the starburst of the initial spread of the virus was examined, it was stated that many infections happened simultaneously in Africa and New York. For that to be possible without human involvement, this monkey would have had to have wings and would have to bite, scratch and or infect many people at the same time. One way to infect multiple people at the same time would be through mass inoculations. Hepatitis B vaccines produced from African chimpanzees were given to Africans and a select gay population in New York City. As it is written, "Let us deal wisely with this people, lest war break out and they join with our enemies". (Exodus 1v10) There are certain powerful entities that have publicly stated that it is in America's best interest if there is a major depopulation of people of African descent.

CHEMICALLY ENGINEERED HOMOSEXUALITY

One thing we have to understand about this bio-warfare is that it is not confined to the individual who receives the tainted vaccines. These ingredients will alter your bio-make up and pass along your ailments and traits for ailments to your offspring. Many black people are now carriers for the sickle cell trait. If they happen to procreate with someone else who has the trait, they will produce a child who has sickle cell, even though neither one of them had it. These are the effects of a bio-makeup that was altered by the mercury contained in the vaccines.

In the earlier days of my biblical studies, my mentor, Elder Yachov used to say "be careful how you hear, what you hear". This was a cautionary word even against the under priests in his own organization. I later found this cautionary word to be very valuable. I was once listening to one of my elder's under priests speak on how people were not born homosexual, they were that way because they made a choice. I immediately thought, there are people born without arms, there are people born without the use of their brain, and then there are people that have more access to their brain than the rest of us and are super intelligent. How can we determine how someone can and cannot be born?

Remember, it was stated earlier on how mercury alters the hormones of people that are exposed to it. We know that there are different hormones that women have and that they differ from the hormones that men have. Remember the focus of the last few chapters, the biblical account of the Hebrews multiplying in Egypt. It was stated to kill the male children. This would keep them from reproducing. When we consider the enormous way in which the homosexual community has grown in numbers we have to wonder, was it by natural means? Today kids are professing their nature to become another gender as early as 7 years old. These things were unheard of when I was growing up. There was a time that I didn't even consider the difference between boys and girls because I threw mud pies at them both. I learned quickly that you couldn't hit girls like you could boys so I immediately didn't want to play with them. I wanted to play with people I could knock upside the wall and they wouldn't cry, but in turn would push me down a hill. Yeah, I know; sick childhood right? But that's the simple thought process of a child. We never had gender thoughts or discussions. With this new information on the table, we have to consider that this may have been the design of certain additives being administered unto us as children, who would then grow up and pass these altered traits on to our children. Keep in mind; if the focus is on the population growth of a certain people, altering their hormones would produce a stagnated growth rate as homosexuals will not procreate. This is a form a bio-weaponry as the males are killed off by simply erasing the desire to create them.

NO MAN NO PROBLEM

Family altering incentives were introduced to assist black women financially if they didn't have a spouse. This incentive allows the woman to reproduce but discourages her from having a stable relationship. Breaking down the family structure is a key element to controlling its population. If the housing authority discovers that the female who is receiving assistance has a man staying with her on a long term basis, she will lose her housing assistance. This drastically decreases the value of a male in such scenarios. In this instance a male is used to create the child but is less important after conception is accomplished. This is an old slavery concept that is still alive and well in slave states. In Georgia, it is still law that the mother and the slave master have all the rights to the newly born child. Georgia law still degrades the power and presence of the man in this day and time. Today a man in Georgia can pay child support and still not be granted visitation rights. My firstborn son was born when I was 21 years old and before me and his mother were married. This means that he was born out of wedlock, or outside of marriage. According to law, my child belonged to his mother and the state of Georgia. So twenty-one years ago I spent $1000 to pay a lawyer for the legitimizing process. If this was not completed, I would have never had any say so whatsoever in any of the decisions concerning my firstborn son. What a system!

THE TORAH TEST

Today there are several different books that are used by various Jewish organizations. These books are post Torah as it pertains to their creation and are admittedly written by men whose only authorization is that they were priests in their respective organizations. These books define rituals and practices that cannot be found in the Torah, which is questionable in itself, seeing that the Torah predates all of these writings. The Torah is no doubt the confirmation of the Hebrews as the chosen people of the God of Israel. With that being said, we must examine the Torah prophesies concerning the plight of the children of Israel.

It is difficult for many people to understand how the troubles of a group of people can be prophesied and set in motion generations before its ultimate fulfillment. When we deal with the troubles prophesied to come upon the children of Israel we find pin point details concerning them being dispersed, their retrieval, and the prophesied doom among many nations who will refuse to acknowledge them for who they are. If the concept of how YHWH the GOD of Israel punishes Israel his people is not understood, none of the prophecies will make sense. Israel was created to be servants to YHWH. If this role was not fulfilled in its entirety, the role of being a servant would still be fulfilled, but it would be fulfilled by Israel becoming servants to men, and more specifically, the heathens. This is laid out specifically in the Torah (The first five books of the Bible). Deuteronomy 28v47 states "…Because thou servedst not YHWH thy God with joyfulness, and with gladness of heart, for the abundance of all *things;* Therefore shalt thou serve thine enemies which YHWH shall send against thee". This key detail outlines why the children of Israel are constantly ending up in situations where they are the servants of another nation. This detail of servitude explains the entire four hundred plus year period of the judges. The period of the judges come directly after the death of Joshua whose predecessor was Moses. Judges chapter 3v7 says "…the children of Israel did evil in the sight of YHWH, and forgat YHWH their Elohim and served Baalim and the groves. Therefore he sold them into the hands of Mesopotamia eight years". This exact scenario repeats itself over and over again. Most people have heard of the seventy year captivity but have no idea that Israel has undergone the same form of captivity repeatedly. The difference is that the severity of those captivities began to increase drastically as time went on. These captivities would eventually culminate into the horrors written about in the Torah.

Deuteronomy chapter 28 discusses the blessings and the curses that would befall the children of Israel. Today most people place all of their attention and emphasis on the blessings. They then look over the earth and take into account the ethnicities which have financial advantage. They then use that as a verification of a people's blessedness. The problem with that scenario is that there are blessings and curses detailed in Deuteronomy chapter 28, and you cannot deal with one without the other. In fact, the curses are more of an indication of what defines the people of Israel more than anything else. Only fourteen verses of Deuteronomy chapter 28 detail the blessings of Israel. The other 54 verses in Deuteronomy chapter 28 directly detail the horrors of the curses. This enormous amount of attention placed on the curses and the effects there of, justifies the curses as an identifier of the true children of Israel. In other words, instead of attempting to find the most financially equipped people on the earth, we should be looking at the people whose plight is littered with captivities. The details of their suffrage are clearly listed before us. Verse 37 of Deuteronomy details that the children of Israel would become 'an astonishment, a byword, and a proverb among all the nations where he shall lead them'. This detail explains that the true children of Israel would most likely not even be called Israel but instead called some byword or proverb given to them by whatever country ruled over them at that time.

THE TERMS OF
UN-ENDEARMENT

America is known as the great melting pot of various ethnicities of people. When we examine the backgrounds of the various ethnicities in America, we find that the background of the so-called African Americans stand out far from the rest. This reason is because this so-called African American is the only ethnic group that was brought here against his will. All other groups came to America for a better life. This so-called African American was brought here to America for the worst life a person can have. This so-called African American began a life in America void of rights, void of freedom, and void of a voice in which to mention what he does not possess. I must explain why I use the term, (so-called African American). The people who were brought here to be the unpaid builders of America have been called by several titles. We have been called Negroes which is a Spanish term for black. The reason for this is because it was the Spanish ships that brought the slaves to America for the most part. We have been called colored, blacks, Afro-Americans, and most recently, African Americans. With this constant title change it is no wonder that this so-called African American has somewhat of an identity crisis here in America. This identity crisis is multiplied when you consider that black people were the only ethnic group that was classified by a hair style. The Afro was a popular hair style, but when its popularity faded so did the title. When the title of African American was introduced, many people hated it. Many people felt no connection to Africa whatsoever but eventually it was accepted, after all, it was better than being classified by a haircut!

Verse 26 of Deuteronomy details how the dead bodies of true Israel would become meat for the fowls of the air. In America specifically, people of color hung by trees as an example for anyone else who dared to be disobedient. So their bodies were purposely left dangling from trees and of course the fowls or birds came to eat the flesh. These events are documented by white Americans as they posed with smiles for pictures next to a lynched person of color.

Verse 30 of Deuteronomy chapter 28 details how a man will be married or set to be married to a woman, only to have another man lie with that woman. These things repeatedly happen to people of color as slave masters and their associates lay with whom they pleased. Also if the slave master believed that mating two specific slaves would create a stronger child slave, those people would be put together, regardless if they were married to someone else.

Verse 32 of Deuteronomy chapter 28 details how the sons and daughters of the children of Israel would be given to another people. To this day, a term of endearment used among so-called African Americans is the term of brother when referring to a male, and sister when referring to a female. These terms have a greater meaning than most people are aware of. During slavery the sons and daughters were often sold to other families. Often times the siblings would see their brother or sister leave with a man and never see them again. Their brother or sister may have been sent across the street or across the country. This term of endearment expressed the question in their hearts as to whether this person in front of them just might be the brother or sister that was taken away from them when they were children.

Verse 36 of Deuteronomy chapter 28 details how the children of Israel would be brought to a land that they knew not. The areas surrounding Israel was always known to them. The children of Israel frequently fled to the areas around Mesopotamia and even further down into Africa on their own. We must remember that Israel walked into Egypt. So these are areas that were known to them. The Trans-Atlantic Slave Trade spread people of color all across the globe, and of course these were places that they knew nothing of. Another key point to mention is that it states that they would be brought to these unknown places, and not that they would flee to these places themselves.

Verse 48 of Deuteronomy chapter 28 details how the children of Israel would be made to serve in nakedness and in hunger and have a yoke of iron placed around their necks. We still have pictures that show how slaves were made to wear a yoke of iron like an animal and plow the ground. In those very depictions we also see the rags they were given for clothes. The eating practices of black Americans today still show how they were forced to work in hunger. Today many so-called African Americans eat pig feet, pig intestine or chitterlings and other parts of the pig that were labeled as undesirable to the slave masters. These abominable practices have become tradition because the slaves ate 'low on the hog', or the worst parts of the hog, while the slave masters ate 'high on the hog', or the good parts of the hog; as if there is such a thing as a good part of a hog!

Verse 49 of Deuteronomy chapter 28 gives details about the nation that would come from far to make siege against Israel. This nation is described using the phrase as swift as the eagle flies. The symbol of Rome and America is the eagle.

Verse 64 of Deuteronomy chapter 28 states how the children of Israel would be scattered all over the globe among other people. It is also stated they would be made to serve other gods. This means that as we listed before, the true children of Israel would not be called Israel, and now we see that they would not worship as Israel should either as an effect of the curse. Verse 65 goes on to state how the children of Israel would find no ease amongst the nations to which they are led. It is important to note that the descendants of slaves in other countries are undergoing similar issues that the so-called African Americans are suffering in America today.

Verse 68 of Deuteronomy chapter 28 states how the children of Israel shall go into Egypt again by way of ships. We must understand that Egypt refers to bondage as it also states that they would be sold as bondmen and bondwomen. The manner of passage is also very important to note as the details state that Israel shall get to this new place of bondage by way of ships where they would not know the language. We know that the Trans-Atlantic Slave Trade's vehicle was the long distance ship. It is also listed that you shall see it no more again. This lets us know that these descriptions are describing the final captivity!

Examining Deuteronomy directly leads us to the Prophet Joel and the prophecies concerning the re-establishment of Israel as a nation. Joel 3 says "…in those days and in that time, when I shall bring again the captivity of Judah and Jerusalem". Bring again means cause to cease, so this is speaking of the ending of all of Israel's captivities. Verse 2 of Joel 3 says that he "will bring all nations down to the valley of Jehoshaphat and plead with them there". This means war. At the ending of verse 2 he says he is pleading or warring with them because 'they have parted his land and scattered Israel among the nations'. So the belief that Israel can become a nation after coming out of only one nation cannot be supported with scripture. Also there has to be a great war of all nations, not a few days' spat between a few countries, to give rebirth to the nation of Israel.

Verse 3 of Joel chapter 3 states that 'they have cast lots for his people Israel and have given a boy for a harlot and sold a girl for wine'. Recently there was a mini-series called The Book of Negroes which showed so-called Jews owning slaves, not being slaves. It was also shown how the Africans (Sons of Ham) sold so-called African Americans (descendants of Shem) for cognac and other trinkets. This directly fits what is written in scripture.

Verse 4 of Joel chapter 3 lists the co-conspirators of this dastardly deed. Verse 4 lists Tyre, Zidon (Sidon) and all the coasts of Palestine. If in depth research is not done at this point, most will see Palestine and automatically attribute these events to a certain group of people. Upon further research we find that Tyre and Zidon (Sidon) are constantly mentioned together. The prophets Jeremiah and Ezekiel mention them together on a constant basis. Zidon is a place in Palestine but we must remember that Israel was called Canaan land before it was called Israel. The reason for this is simple. The people who lived there before Israel were Canaanites or more specifically the people we know as Africans. Genesis Chapter 10 says...and the sons of Ham, which means hot or burnt as we mentioned in earlier chapters, were Cush or Ethiopia, Mizraim and Phut or Egyptians and Canaan. All of these are so-called African tribes and are black in color. Genesis chapter 10 and verse 15 says "...Canaan begat Zidon(*Sidon*) his first born". The first kingdoms to rule on the earth were African and that is confirmed both by the Bible and secular historical writings. So now we have clearer understanding of what group of people is being mentioned in verse 4. Tyre, Zidon(Sidon) and all the coast of Palestine is referring to the Canaanites or Africans. With that now being understood, let's examine what was prophesied concerning their actions against the children of Israel.

Verse 6 of Joel chapter 3 states "...the children of Judah and Jerusalem have you sold unto the Grecians". When we examine the history of the slave trade, we find that Africans sold slaves to the Greeks or gentile nations. Earlier mis-information about slavery's origin listed it as if the gentiles went to Africa and captured people, when the truth is far from that. The gentiles could have never bought what was not up for sale. To add to that point, when George W. Bush, the son, took office, there was this belief that he would apologize for slavery. That did not happen, but what did happen is that he stated we all had our part in that. The Africans sold the tribes of people who sojourned among them. To this day, there is very little interaction between Africans and so-called African Americans. The ending of verse 6 states that in doing this, Israel has been removed far from their border! It is also interesting to note that this term of "African" is a very broad term. There are many people who are residing in Africa and are called Africans, but are Hebrews by ethnicity. The Lemba tribe is just one of those groups. The DNA of the Lemba tribe was tested and it was found that their DNA showed a large and definite connection to ancient Israelites. Their DNA showed a larger connection to ancient Israelites than the people who currently reside in Israel today. Imagine that!

Verse 7 of Joel chapter 3 says "...I will raise them out of the places where you have sold them". This in itself verifies that Israel for the most part are still captives in the lands where they are currently located. What further proves this is the condition that the earth will be in when this prophesied war of ALL the heathens take place. Verse 15 states that the sun and the moon shall withdraw their shining. We know that the same things are stated in the New Testament book of Revelation, and we have no documentation of any such event ever happening before. So according to the prophecies in the old and new testaments, it is impossible for Israel to already have returned to the land. Verse 17 states that strangers shall pass through her no more. At this present time there are mosques, synagogues and Christian churches almost touching one another. These things ought not to be!

Frequently when this sort of evidence is presented, people go through great lengths to discredit the information, all the while not presenting any information of their own. I challenge anyone who claims to be the descendants of the ancient Israelites to produce the historical evidence of their past and match it up to the events contained in the Torah, Tanakh, and the New Testament.

JEW-LIKE

The origin of ish

Ish is a suffix used to form adjectives from nouns, which means "with the sense of belonging to" or "having the characteristics of", or simply meaning "like". To be British, English or Spanish basically means belonging to Britain, England, or Spain in the sense of having the characteristics of Britain, England, or Spain. The difference here is these are countries. When we get to the term "Jew" we understand that it is a term that has become to be known to denote a certain group of people. Here the term Jew already denotes the people, so why add the suffix "ish", which then means 'like a Jew'.

Blackish

There is a very popular television show entitled "Blackish". The entire setup of the show is based upon black people who have attained financial success and have moved to an affluent neighborhood. This move has caused their kids to grow up without encountering the same things that normal black kids face. They constantly undergo comical situations in which they question their own blackness because of their current status. So the title of the show is black-ish, because they are black in look but not black in a sense of the everyday struggle of black people, so they are "blackish" or "black- like".

THE ANTI-SEMITIC CONTROVERSY

The term anti-Semitic means anti-Shemitic. Shem is one of the sons of Noah, from whom the ancient Israelites are derived. Anti-Semitic is a term used to denote hatred and bigotry against so-called Jews. So to understand it clearly, when someone asks if you are anti-Semitic, they only want to know your views about so-called Jews. They are not concerned if you have hatred and bigotry against any other people in the world, just so-called Jews. So the term is against racism, but only certain types of racism.

The irony is, the majority of the people asking about anti-Semitism and or claiming it amongst other people, are not actually Semites themselves. The majority of the people who ask this amongst other people are converts who have converted to Judasim and have kept it for several generations, but are actually gentiles according to their ancestral lineage.

Let us add more biblical history to this portion of the discussion. After repeated disobedience against the God of Israel, Israel was split into two nations. One nation was called Yehudah or Judah, and the other portion was called Israel. Yehudah or Judah was eventually comprised of three tribes. The three tribes of the nation of Yehudah or Judah were Benjamin, Judah and Levi. The nation of Israel was comprised of the other nine tribes. The tribe of Yehudah or Judah was the tribe of the kings while the tribe of Levi was the tribe of the priests. These were the two most powerful tribes in all of Israel. As documented by 2 Kings chapter 17v18 "...YHWH was angry with Israel and removed them out of his sight: none was left but the tribe or house of Judah only", which was comprised of Benjamin, Judah and Levi. Israel as a whole has always had a problem with assimilating with other nations and cultures, but this problem is about to be magnified tremendously by what happens next. As documented by 2 Kings chapter 17v23-24… "Israel (*the 9 tribes*), were carried away to Assyria. The king of Assyria then brought men from Babylon, and from Cuthah, and from Ava, and from Hamath, and from Sepharvaim and placed them in the cities of Samaria instead of the children of Israel". This situation has now introduced foreign nations into the culture and the land of Israel, but the intermingling is about to get much deeper. The newly introduced people had problems in the land because they knew not the manner of the God of Israel. As documented by 2 Kings Chapter 17v27 "…the king of Assyria commanded them to carry one of the priests whom they took away from there; and let him teach you the manner of the God of the land. So one of the priests came and taught them how to fear the God of Israel". These nations were taught how to fear the God of Israel but what's written lets us know they did just enough to get by, meaning they mingled their prior pagan customs with the culture of Israel. This is confirmed by what is written in 2 Kings Chapter

17v32 "...they feared YHWH but made to themselves the lowest of men to be priests, so they feared YHWH, but served their own gods". To this day there are Jewish people who trace their connection back to being Sephardic. Sephardic is of Sepharvaim, which are converts and not actual descendants of Israel. So they are" Jew-like" or "Jewish", but they are not Jews.

To understand this we must examine what the bible says about the children of Israel and them being dispersed throughout the countries. Notice I said, countries and not country. Today we have been told that the Jews suffered great tragedy in Germany and was thus given land in Israel as a result of the tragedy that they suffered. There are already books that go into great detail detailing how this is not so, but as this is not our true focus, we will move on. The prophet Isaiah mentions the large scale event that will eventually place Israel back into their homeland. Isaiah Chapter 11v11 says "...And it shall come to pass in that day, that YHWH shall set his hand again the second time to recover the remnant of his people that are left from Assyria, and Egypt, and from Pathros, and Cush (Ethiopia), and from Elam and Shinar, from Hamath and the islands of the sea". Verse 12 of Isaiah says he "will gather the dispersed of Yehudah (Judah) from the four corners of the earth". We have been told that all the so-called Jews came from one place to inhabit the land of Israel. This cannot be backed up by scripture and is therefore a complete fallacy!

Please don't get the wrong idea and believe that the God of Israel does not allow other nations to become a part of Israel and its culture. From the beginning the Torah states that if a man wants to keep the Passover, he must be circumcised and he can participate as one born in the land. Another situation is documented in the book of Esther where other people became Jews. Esther Chapter 8v17 says "...and many of the people of the land became Jews". These are two biblically proven occurrences where other nations became a part of Israel. One of them involves priests from other nations who then became "Jew-like priests" who mingled their previous paganism with Israelite culture. When we fast forward to what is happening today as other books have been introduced as having just as much authenticity as the Torah, one has to wonder how did this happen? These books have rituals and stories that don't agree with the practices and stories that are written in the Torah.

In the book of Revelation it is written about the declining condition of the church. In the midst of dealing with the condition of the church, it is also written in Revelation Chapter 3v9 "...I know the blasphemy of them which say they are Jews, and are not, but are the synagogue of Satan". True Israel would never be allowed to worship other Gods without the punishment of captivity. The proselytes or converts were given more leeway to transgress the culture and ways of the God of Israel.

BOASTING AGAINST THE BRANCHES

As was clearly stated earlier, other nations were and are allowed to grab a hold onto the doctrine and ways of the God of Israel. In fact, it is written that his house shall be a house of prayer for all people. Due to the breaking of the covenant, natural Israel as a whole would undergo hardships of captivity. This leaves and allows converted nations to worship and practice the culture of Israel without hindrance. This has caused many converts to deny natural Israel because of their absence from the land. In Romans 11v1, the apostle Paul felt the need to write about the state of Israel. He wrote "...has God cast away his people? God forbid, for I am also an Israelite, of the seed of Abraham, of the tribe of Benjamin". Today everyone claims to be a Jew, although this term referred to the people of the tribe of Judah or of the divided nation of Judah. There are twelve tribes of Israel, not twelve tribes of Judah, so it is virtually impossible for everyone to be Jews. The apostle Paul also warns the gentiles not to boast against Israel, who are the natural branches. He says…I speak to you gentiles in as much as I am the apostle of the gentiles. The apostle Paul writes that the gentiles were grafted into Israel's tree and says in Romans Chapter 11v18 "…boast not against the branches". He also wrote that "blindness in part has happened unto Israel until the fullness of the gentiles be come in". The fullness of the gentiles is their prophesied time to rule the earth. This time was given to the prophet Daniel concerning the great image of gold. At the end of the gentile rule, the kingdom is then placed into the hands of Israel.

There are prophesied events that must take place before the ancient Israelites are allowed to re-enter the land of Israel. Those stipulations do not, and have not applied to converts. In other words, converts or proselytes would be allowed to halfway serve, while true descendants would not!

THE CLOSING

If we are going to examine any issue, we must analyze the facts without emotional attachments and partiality. If we believe we already know the answer before we examine the evidence, we will allow emotion to draw out the conclusion that we already had previously before the discussion began.

Most will say that it is a great thing to be the natural descendants of the ancient Israelites, and indeed it is a welcome feeling after being treated as second class citizens for all of your natural life. Here is where the immediate joy ends. As we realize what the prophecy says about how the true natural descendants of Israel would be scattered all over the world, we must think about how horrific that forced migration was. The details of the Trans-Atlantic Slave Trade have been documented as just that, horrific and deplorable. Now we have to understand that the true natural descendants of the twelve tribes of Israel will be forced to undergo another forced migration back to the land of Israel. This forced migration will not be directly to Israel, as the nations will not accept this so-called Negro for who he really is. This is why YHWH says he will have to "plead with the nations for his heritage Israel" (Ref. Joel 3v2). This is somewhat understandable as many offspring of converts and proselytes have grown up believing that it is their heritage and theirs alone; this added to the fact that the nations, for the most part have accepted the converted proselytes as being Israel, or more specifically, the Jews.

To completely understand the terms Jew and Israel we must mention a few things. Most people only recognize the term Jew as being the name of the Holy people. This term is misleading on a variety of levels. First of all, the bible states that Jacob was named Israel. His twelve sons make up the twelve tribes of Israel and were thus called the

Israelites. One of those tribes was named after the fourth born son Yehudah, which is called Judah today. The nation of Israel was constantly disobedient unto YHWH and was eventually split into two nations, a northern and a southern kingdom. One kingdom became known as Israel, which consisted of nine of the twelve tribes and was cut off and disciplined first. While the other kingdom was called Yehudah, or Judah in English, consisted of three tribes. Being of the kingly tribe and kingdom is a great thing, but there are not twelve tribes of Yehudah (Judah), so theoretically, physically, and spiritually, it is impossible for everyone of Israel to be a so-called Jew! The term Jew comes from the English term Judah, which is newly derived. Knowing that the term Jew (Yehudi or plural, Yehudim) only refers to one small portion of Israel, being the southern kingdom, it is amazing that most of the people who occupy the land of Israel currently, say that there is no need to look for any other tribes. Consider if you had a family of twelve brothers in your family and nine of your brothers were lost, would you truly say that there is no need to look for them? Consider what the wisest man that ever lived said when uttering righteous judgment concerning two women and one living child. Both women claimed that the living child was theirs and the dead child was the other one's. King Solomon ordered to have the baby cut in half and to be divided amongst them. One woman said, "Ok do it", but the other woman said, "Don't harm the child, just give her the baby". King Solomon then proceeded to give the baby to the woman that was willing to give the baby up to save its life. He stated that she was indeed the baby's mother. His great wisdom shows that there is no measuring what someone will do for someone they love. So the mere thought that there is no need to look for lost tribes, could not come from someone who has love for their family.

We have to also examine the possibility that a major portion of the population of natural descendants of Israel will not want to leave the lands that they are in. It is also customary that after long captivities, a large amount of Israel would not want to return to their homeland, especially if they have no remembrance of it. We must remember the account of the children of Israel coming out of Egypt. This deportation was not pleasant at all! The sentiment went from not wanting to let the Israelites go, to get them out of here immediately. The change of mindset came about as Egypt began to suffer because of Israel. Every day these scattered peoples who are not just among America, but are among almost every nation under heaven, are finding themselves of less and less value among the countries where they have been scattered. Constant news stories of people of color committing crimes are plastered across the television. These stories help create the mindset that these countries are suffering too much at the hands of people of color. These same tactics were used over and over immediately following the so-called abolishment of slavery. Newspaper articles stating black brute raped a white woman were printed falsely and led to race riots all over North America. We are not talking about the finding of the so-called guilty individual, but we are talking about white mobs going through the streets and killing every black person they saw; burning all of their property and eventually taking their land. Most black people believe that if they go to school and get a good job that these things won't affect them. The problem with that thought process is historically, when the mobs of whites reacted to the false news stories, they came to kill and burn down the houses of the wealthy elite blacks who had not committed any crimes in their entire lives. In some cases entire towns were burned down and people fled because of false news stories.

Meanwhile, when Caucasians are arrested, these incidents are not aired everyday on the evening news, giving the impression that Caucasians are not committing crimes.

We must consider the recent mass killing by Dylan Roof. He was a white supremacist who killed unarmed black church goers during their bible study. This event was meant to spearhead a race war by his own admission. This event was supposed to prompt a revenge attack by some black person or some black group. The problem was, no black people took the bait. Evil actions such as these are meant to bring regular people into their fight. I must be clear though, although there are many atrocities committed against people of color, the ultimate entity in charge of it all is the God of Israel. Israel was told that they would be punished seven times more for their sins (Leviticus 26v18). Israel was also told that if they did not serve YHWH, they would have to serve as bondmen in other people's land. In other words, either serve the GOD of Israel, or you will become slaves in other people's land.

SNARED IN HOLES & HID IN PRISON HOUSES

The prophet Isaiah spoke about Israel's state of being, saying 'they are snared in holes and all hid in prison houses'. The constant title changes of so-called African Americans displayed that America was unsure on how to deal with its former slaves. This is evident by the various race riots and the prison system, which got its boost immediately following the so-called abolishment of slavery. After slavery was no more, there came a need for the powers-that-be to constantly monitor the dealings of these newly freed people. New laws were passed to specifically restrict the movement and development of black people and their communities.

BLACK CODES

After the civil war was lost by the Confederate south, a set of laws called the Black Codes were enacted by southern states. These laws made it possible for African Americans to have certain rights, such as ownership of property, but true rights were severely limited. Black people were not allowed to testify against whites, or to serve on juries. Black people were denied the right to vote, or start a job without the approval of the previous employer. This small detail basically forced African Americans to continue working for an individual unless he allowed them to leave, so basically it was slavery in another form.

"Pig Laws" unfairly penalized poor African Americans for crimes such as stealing a farm animal. Please understand, since blacks could not testify against whites, if you were accused, you were automatically guilty! Vagrancy laws made it a crime to be unemployed. So an African-American could be arrested and imprisoned if his former owners did not hire him. Black people would often face stiff penalties and long prison sentences for the same minor infractions that whites were only reprimanded for.

CONVICT LEASING

Convict leasing was a system that allowed the leasing out of prisoners to private companies that paid the state a certain fee in return. Convicts worked for private owned companies during the day outside the prison and returned to their cells at night. This system was made to look just, I mean after all they were convicts, but in actuality it was 'slavery in a dress'. Eventually convict leasing was deemed immoral so it was replaced by deplorable state-run chain gangs. This system, although revamped and repackaged, is basically still alive and well today.

Today's corporations can lease factories inside of privately owned prisons. Several large private corporations are running a conglomerate of prisons-for-profit, which explains America's need to lock somebody up. America, the so-called land of the free, imprisons more people than any other country in the world! The United States imprisons 25% of the world's prisoners but make up only 5% of the world's people. The prison system has allowed America to have third world sweat shop factories which are able to compete with under developed countries, producing products without paying the workers, all the while being able to display, MADE IN AMERICA on the label!

The states have made deals with private prison corporations to keep the prisons stocked. If the private prison is not completely stocked with prisoners, the states will have to pay a penalty for not providing enough prisoners. Laws such as three strikes and mandatory sentencing is just a few ways to ensure that the privately owned, wall street invested prisons are constantly, in the black.

This so-called African American is hid in prison houses with the help of colored laws that pinpoint and penalize with a bias. But we must remember what is written concerning Israel, "You shall be punished seven times more for your sins". One such example is a Federal law that stipulated five years imprisonment without possibility of parole for possession of 5 grams of crack cocaine and 10 years for possession of less than 2 ounces of crack or rock-cocaine. We must add into this equation that crack cocaine is a type of poor man's cocaine. It was developed by a chemist and marketed to poor black communities. On the other hand, a sentence of 5 years for cocaine powder requires possession of 500 grams, which is 100 times more than the quantity of rock cocaine for the same sentence. Most of those who use cocaine powder are white, middle-class or rich people, while mostly blacks and Latinos use rock-cocaine, because crack was created, developed, and manufactured with poor communities in mind. This colored law ensures that the prison system would be packed with black drug offenders and gives the impression that blacks were involved with drugs more than whites; and that is grossly incorrect.

When people hear presidential campaigns that proclaim that they will block foreign businesses and bring commerce back to the United States, people assume that everyday Americans will be able to get this work. It never does occur to them that this work may not be available to law abiding citizens as it is more profitable for businesses to use cheap prison labor to manufacture their products. This affects black people so white America is not concerned, but eventually, with the constant growth of prisons and rise of unjust laws targeted towards so-called African-Americans; this epidemic will eventually affect white America, as the prison labor force will eventually take the jobs of white people.

Even though we are disproportionately dying by the hands of the police, the police are not the cause of the problem. The police are the overseers in this new slave system. The overseer only does what the slave master allows. If the slave master insisted that he not harm his workers, the overseer, or officer is forced to comply. When African Americans are killed by the police, more often than not, the officer is only punished with paid administrative leave, which is in fact a vacation.

If you open up the prison houses, you will find an enormous amount of people of color, not people who call themselves the Jews. In fact, many of the people who call themselves Jews, also owned slaves. Even in the land of Israel, people of color are constantly degraded as lesser-valued individuals. The ironic part of this is that the Ethiopian Jews who have been called Falasha, are accepted among so-called Israelis but must convert to the Israeli form of Judaism. How can it be possible for one group of dark skinned people to be accepted as being Israel? Meanwhile we are told that no other group of colored people could possibly be Israelites. The issue is, the Ethiopian connection cannot be denied. The historian Josephus wrote about the destruction of Israel and stated that Titus killed 1.2 million Yehudim (Jews) and sold the rest to work in the salt mines of Africa. This historical document-ation verifies how Israelites were forced into African culture and society. We are to believe that jet black Ethiopians can be the brothers of the white Israelis, but no other black people could possibly be. The truth is, the historian Josephus explains how Israelites were forced in to Africa, and the prophet Joel explains how they were forced out. Joel Chapter 3v4 talks about Tyre and Zidon. When we examine the lineage of both Tyre and Zidon we find that these are descendants of Ham who are so-called Africans today. In verse 6 of Joel, it goes on to state how these Africans sold the children of Yehudah (Judah) to the Greeks or rather the gentiles. When we examine the Trans-Atlantic Slave Trade routes, we find there was a slave port called the Fort of Quidah (*French*) or Yehudah. Why was there a slave fort named after Yehudah or Judah in Africa? I challenge anyone to find a documented event in history that details the so-called Jews being sold by Africans to Caucasians! Also you must also look at the events associated with the writing in Joel 3. The selling of these people has to happen after the slavery in Egypt and according to the prophet, it won't be rectified until the great battle of all nations.

If the prophets proclaim that the judgment for these things will not be completed until the battle of Armageddon, how do we have a state of

Israel at this present time? Did the prophets lie? Were the prophets mistaken, or were we all sold a bill of goods? YHWH stated that his house shall be an house of prayer for all peoples. All means all, not all except certain people who look a particular way.

I hope this writing finds you in peace.

Shalom

Priest Esaac Ben Israel

SOURCES:

Origin of Aids - Leonard Horowitz, DMD., MA., M.P.H.

Scoefield Study Bible

Apocrypha- Cambridge University Press

Strong's Bible Dictionary

CNN

GPBS- (GA Public Broadcasting)

The Wars of the Jews – Josephus Flavius

Robert Kennedy – Deadly Immunity

Elder Priest Yachov Ben Yisrael – Too many to List

Book and cover design: Samuel Okike.

BIOGRAPHY

ESAAC ISRAEL was born in Atlanta, GA. but moved to Decatur, GA in his elementary years. Raised by a single mother, he was no stranger to hard work. He got his first job when he was 14 years old. He was also no stranger to trouble. He was kicked out of four of the five different high schools he attended. After barely graduating high school, he quickly turned things around and attended Devry Institute of Technology and received an Associates Degree in Electronics. He graduated from Devry when he was twenty years old and purchased his first home at the age of twenty two.

He has performed as a stand up comedian and has recorded two rap albums. He says that those minor accomplishments pale in comparison to meeting his mentor and teacher, Elder Priest Yachov Ben Yisrael. He has appeared on television and radio programs and have written countless documentaries while under Yachov's tutelage. He was the coordinator for all Audio/Visual media under Elder Priest Yachov. He trained on the priesthood under Elder Priest Yachov for seven years. He says he never would have approached the priesthood if his teacher was still alive. The passing of his mentor pushed him into the priesthood. He is now the Head Priest at The United Congregation of Israel in Stone Mountain, GA. He says his whole life changed when he met his mentor, and he has dedicated his life to serving the lost sheep in hopes that one day, he can do the same thing that his elder did for him.